PATHWISE®
FRAMEWORK COMPONENT
MINICOURSES FOR TEACHERS

QUESTIONING TO ENHANCE
STUDENT LEARNING

Acknowledgments

As the author of this minicourse, I would like to thank Educational Testing Service (ETS) for the opportunity to complete such gratifying work. In concert with the Teaching and Learning Division at ETS, I would also like to thank the following outstanding educators for their dialogue on the teaching component presented in this book: Lisa Baatz, Debra Baer, Katherine Bassett, Susan Black, Linda Brach, Lynn Bridge, Susan Cooper, Elaine Harbison, Lee Ann Kovalak, Barbara LaSaracina, Colleen Seiler Mula, Rosalyn Payne, Karen Price, Ernie Read, Linda Smith, Toni Watt, and Jan Wilson. We hope that their professional knowledge and experiences will be useful to other educators.

Teaching and Learning Division

Educational Testing Service
MS 18-D
Rosedale Road
Princeton, NJ 08541-0001
Web site: http://www.ets.org/pathwise

ISBN 0-88685-209-9

Printed in the United States of America

07 06 05 04 03 02   10 9 8 7 6 5 4 3 2 1

Contents

PART IV: TRYING NEW QUESTIONING TECHNIQUES IN YOUR CLASSROOM

PART V: REFLECTING, ASSESSING, AND PLANNING FUTURE ADVANCEMENT

APPENDICES

To Administrators:
PATHWISE® Minicourses for Teachers

The Teaching and Learning Division of Educational Testing Service (ETS®) has developed a series of minicourses to support the growing number of teaching professionals who are engaged in continuous inquiry on their own or through school-level, peer-supported, self-directed professional development programs, such as the PATHWISE®: Framework Portfolio Program.

PATHWISE Minicourses are research-based, skill-specific guides to improving key components of professional teaching practice. They are designed to be used by individual teachers or by teachers working collaboratively. While the framework of the minicourses supports processes explored in the Portfolio Program, it is not necessary to know or use the Portfolio Program to benefit from the minicourses.

PATHWISE Minicourses provide teachers with a powerful, structured, self-directed approach to systematically and comprehensively examine, critique, and improve particular elements of individual teaching practice.

Each minicourse:

- **situates** a particular classroom skill in the overall practice of teaching

- **describes** the value of the skill in terms of enhancing student learning

- **provides** a scale that describes various levels of proficiency in the skill

- **points** to resources that particularize the skill by grade level or subject

- **provides** valuable information about using the skill in the classroom

- **offers** opportunities for self-reflection on current skill levels

- **guides** teachers in a step-by-step approach to setting goals for advancing proficiency

- **provides** practical tools and advice for improving skills incrementally in the classroom

- **encourages** ongoing reflection, with the goal of continuously enriching student learning

All PATHWISE Minicourses are grounded in established, professional standards for teaching. They are intended to help individual teachers — and groups of teachers working together — structure their own, self-directed learning, apply this new learning in the classroom, and use student learning as evidence of their growing effectiveness.

PATHWISE Minicourse workbooks are designed to help teachers identify areas for professional growth and to practice their skills in a continuous learning cycle. Teachers use the minicourses to set their own professional goals and to guide themselves in developing and implementing plans to achieve them. One minicourse may be reused several times as teachers continuously and incrementally refine their skills.

TO TEACHERS:
BEFORE YOU BEGIN ...

This PATHWISE Minicourse is designed to help you — a teaching professional interested in advancing your own practice — refine a key professional skill: the use of questioning as an instructional strategy to enhance student engagement, student thinking, and student learning.

Research shows that while questioning is a pervasive practice in most classrooms, the use of *planned* questioning targeted to specific instructional purposes is surprisingly rare. While you may think questioning skill is intuitive — a personal quality teachers simply possess to varying degrees — studies indicate that skill in this key instructional area can be learned and improved.

This minicourse provides information integrated with activities that move in a stepwise fashion toward the preparation and implementation of a lesson supported by planned questions. The minicourse workbook is organized around a learning cycle that can be repeated as you incrementally advance your teaching practice. Related Activities, included at the end of each unit, provide tools to help you use valuable information about a key instructional skill to reflect on your current teaching practice and set your own goals for advancement.

Part I	Understanding the Value of Effective Questioning and Discussion

Effective questioning can help you engage students intellectually and facilitate purposeful discussions that lead students toward learning goals you set. Part I introduces questioning as an instructional strategy and describes proficiency in this area. Related Activities in Part I point you to articles that consider questioning and discussion techniques within the context of your subject and/or instructional grade level. Journal space is provided here to help you reflect on both the articles you read and your current teaching practice.

Part II — Using Different Question Types for Different Instructional Purposes

An understanding of question types can help you reflect on the range of questions you use in your classroom and plan specific ways to improve your questioning skill. Part II of this minicourse presents several ways of looking at question types, as well as the purposes for which different question types are best used. Related Activities at the end of the unit are designed to help you evaluate the range of question types you typically use in your classroom and reflect on question types you would like to try out in Part IV.

Part III — Interpersonal Skills and Climate That Support Questioning and Discussion

Successful use of questioning in the classroom is supported by specific interpersonal skills and classroom environments that encourage students to open up to questions and discussion. Part III addresses these considerations. Related Activities for the Teacher help you reflect on your current communication skills and your classroom environment, set goals for improvement, and begin considering potential obstacles to advancing your level of questioning. Related Activities for Students can help you accustom your students to a questioning environment.

Part IV — Trying New Questioning Techniques in Your Classroom

After you determine the first step you would like to take toward improving your skill with instructional questioning, the next step is to plan and practice a lesson that is supported by questions. Part IV of this minicourse is structured to guide you, step by step, in the development of questions targeted to your instructional goals. You can draw from word banks and sentence stems to draft one level or several levels of questions intended to engage your students in learning objectives you outline. Related Activities in this section are intended to help you reflect on important classroom considerations as you plan.

Part V — Reflecting, Assessing, and Planning Future Advancement

The final section of this minicourse is anything but final. It is as much a beginning as an ending. In Part V you look back on the thoughtful steps you have just taken to enhance your students' learning, but you also look forward to new reflections — and your next step toward improving your questioning skill. Related Activities in Part V guide you in a constructive assessment of what you and your students learned from using new kinds of questions in your classroom. Your assessment doubles as the initial plan for your next incremental advancement.

As you proceed through this workbook, you may want to keep in mind that the same research that validates the effectiveness of planned questioning also notes that developing skill in this area takes time. It is important that you set an incremental goal for yourself and allow yourself ample practice before moving on to the next step. Using questions skillfully is a dynamic process that depends as much on your students as on you. As you rehearse your questioning skills in the classroom, measure how well you are doing by observing your students' reactions. Like a weathervane, your students' responses will direct you to important next questions and teaching directions. Use your on-the-spot assessments of your students' responses to make minor adjustments as you practice — by rephrasing a question or switching to a higher or lower level of questioning, for example.

STANDARDS OF PROFESSIONAL PRACTICE

A set of professional standards provides a common language to talk about teaching. PATHWISE Minicourses rely on the components of good teaching described in *Enhancing Professional Practice: A Framework for Teaching*[1] by Charlotte Danielson. These professional standards are aligned to the principles of the Interstate New Teacher Assessment and Support Consortium as well as other standards for teachers.

In her book, Danielson divides instructional practice into four principal domains with a total of 22 related components. Within this framework, "Using Questioning and Discussion Techniques" is considered a component of Domain 3: Instruction. (To examine a graphic that shows how this component is situated within the larger framework of teaching, see Appendix A.) It is not necessary to know more about this framework to proceed with the minicourse, but if you are interested, information on Danielson's book is provided below.

ABOUT RELATED ACTIVITIES

In all Pathwise Minicourses, Related Activities are intended to help you identify areas for professional growth and to practice your skills in a continuous learning cycle. In Part I of the minicourse — the first stage of the cycle — you gather and reflect on new information and begin to self-assess your practice. Next, after deeper consideration of the skill under discussion — in this case, using questioning in the classroom — you reflect more specifically on your current teaching practice and set an incremental learning goal. In Part III, the third stage, you examine related issues that support the skill and reflect on ways these issues may impact your success as well as student learning. Fourth, you plan and implement a lesson in which you rehearse the skill at a new level. And finally, in Part V, you reflect on your new learning and take notes that may later form the basis of your next incremental advancement.

---

[1]Danielson, C. (1996). *Enhancing professional practice: A framework for teaching*. Alexandria, VA: Association for Supervision & Curriculum Development. Available: http://shop.ascd.org (search by title from this Web page).

THE PATHWISE MINICOURSE LEARNING CYCLE [2]

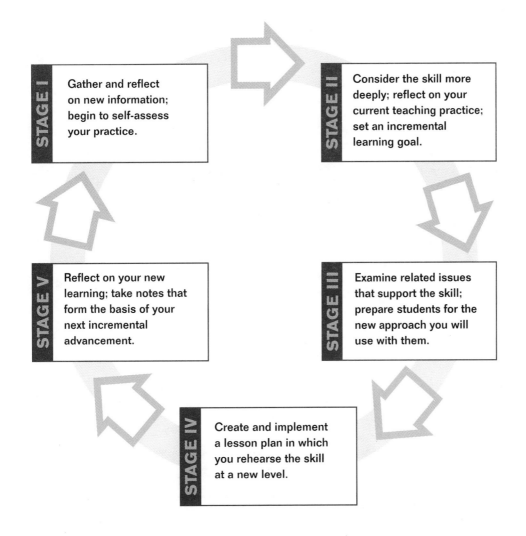

STAGE I — Gather and reflect on new information; begin to self-assess your practice.

STAGE II — Consider the skill more deeply; reflect on your current teaching practice; set an incremental learning goal.

STAGE III — Examine related issues that support the skill; prepare students for the new approach you will use with them.

STAGE IV — Create and implement a lesson plan in which you rehearse the skill at a new level.

STAGE V — Reflect on your new learning; take notes that form the basis of your next incremental advancement.

Your completion of Related Activities should reflect your personal style. For example, some teachers may approach these written activities with more fullness than others, depending on their current levels of proficiency and individual learning styles. It is not essential to use complete sentences; bulleted or numbered phrases may be more helpful to you. However, it is important to document your thoughts and your progress. As you advance your practice, this documentation can serve as an invaluable resource to you as you revisit topics and pursue deeper levels of understanding and application.

Due to the continuous nature of the learning cycle, before you begin you may want to think about how you will collect your responses to activities and your reflections related to this minicourse. For example, you might dedicate a notebook to your responses and use the workbook pages as a guide. Your notebook will serve as your portfolio of progress related to this skill as you use the minicourse workbook multiple times to incrementally refine your practice. Know, however, that the minicourse workbook is designed to be written in, so feel free to take notes in the margin, to highlight points of interest, and to fill in the charts.

---

[2] The Minicourse Learning Cycle parallels the cycle that is presented in other programs in the PATHWISE series: Plan-Teach-Reflect-Apply (PTRA). In Parts 1-3 of this minicourse you *plan*; in Part 4 you *teach*, and in Part 5 you *reflect* on your learning and consider how you might *apply* what you have learned to your future teaching.

PART I

OBJECTIVES:

- UNDERSTAND HOW EFFECTIVE QUESTIONING AND DISCUSSION BENEFIT STUDENTS.

- READ AND REFLECT ON DISCIPLINE- AND GRADE-SPECIFIC BENEFITS OF QUESTIONING STRATEGIES.

QUESTIONS IN THE CLASSROOM

Few instructional skills are as important to good teaching, or as pervasive across classrooms and disciplines, as questioning. Researchers estimate that teachers spend anywhere from a third to more than three quarters of their instructional time asking students questions. One study estimates that teachers ask 300 to 400 questions every day.[3] And yet, little formal training exists to help teachers hone this critical skill.

You may think that interjecting apt and timely questions into an instructional conversation is intuitive — a natural and spontaneous process that cannot be taught. But research[4] on the effectiveness of training in the use of questioning techniques shows that the ability to develop specific questions and multi-level questioning strategies that are targeted to instructional goals can be learned and improved with planning and practice. In other words, while some level of questioning may be natural to most teachers, questioning becomes a more effective teaching strategy when it is employed purposefully. Further, the interpersonal skills and classroom environment that encourage thoughtful responses from students may be cultivated as well.

Effective questioning can help you accomplish many of your instructional goals. For example, you can use a good question to provoke students' curiosity, inspire students to search and experiment, and ignite a rich class discussion. Your well thought-out questions can form the heart of class projects and papers. You can also use questions to check how thoroughly students have prepared for class, to review previously learned material, to facilitate group work, and to assess how well students have learned.

Of course, the same *type* of question cannot serve all of your diverse goals. This minicourse provides information that can help you expand your knowledge of questions and their effects. By using this information in guided reflections and skill practice, you can become more adept at posing questions suited to your specific instructional goals.

---

[3]Leven, T., & Long, R. (1981). *Effective instruction*. Washington, DC: Association for Supervision and Curriculum Development.
[4]*How better questioning leads to improved learning*. Appalachia Regional Educational Laboratory. Available: http://www.ael.org/rel/quilt/questng.htm

THE VALUE OF A GOOD QUESTION

Skilled questioning is one of the most versatile teaching tools in your professional skill set. You can use questions in your classroom for a wide range of instructional purposes. At one end of the spectrum, you can use questions to monitor small groups of students on task as they work on a project ("Has everyone completed part 1 of the assignment?") or to perform a simple readiness check before giving a test ("What is the correct order of operations for equations?"). At the other end, your questions can drive weeks of observation ("What are the best criteria for classifying rocks and minerals?"), experimentation ("What are the properties of aerobic and anaerobic processes?"), and provocative class discussion ("What does the red letter 'A' worn by Hester Prynne in *The Scarlet Letter* tell us about seventeenth-century morality?").

Perhaps the most important reason for using well thought-out questions in the classroom is that questions have extraordinary power to help you engage students intellectually. A carefully framed question communicates to students that you believe in their individual capacities to learn. *What you think is important*, the question says. *You have the power to learn*. Few students can resist the urge to perform to these positive expectations.

Students who are asked thoughtful questions, and who are permitted to discover their own answers, develop a questioning attitude themselves. When students interact with planned questions on a daily basis, they unknowingly rehearse key cognitive processes that can make learning intrinsic. Instead of being passive consumers of knowledge, they learn to locate it, to construct it, and to think beyond it. Before long, they learn to frame their own purposeful questions. When students' own questions are used to drive instruction, they are empowered to continue learning for the rest of their lives.

> *Perhaps the most important reason for using well thought-out questions in the classroom is that questions have extraordinary power to help you engage students intellectually.*

At all levels, questions teach students to make wise independent choices. Although your questions provide students with significant learning cues, these cues do not insult students; they empower them to think and to learn. Well-framed questions enable students to reflect on and use their knowledge purposefully, to weigh choices, and to make informed learning decisions. Helpful questions — such as, "What do you need to know before you can do that?" — do not diminish the pride students feel in arriving at the knowledge they need on their own. Like good stage directions, your questions facilitate student performance from the wings, but when the curtain falls, students step forward to take the bows.

When students begin to internalize the practice of using questions, your role as facilitator — rather than lecturer or deliverer of instruction — increases in importance. When you direct a discussion among classmates with your questions, you help them hear one another and respond to one another with respect. Even students who tend not to be vocal may be willing to enter a democratic, instructional conversation on a topic that is meaningful to them. In hearing their peers' thoughts and questions, students can become more confident about their own.

Questions can also provide you with deeper knowledge of students' abilities. Regular use of questions as an instructional technique permits you to observe students' thinking in action. Student responses indicate their current level of understanding. They also reveal their misconceptions and other obstacles to learning. Unlike written assessments, which often reveal such things after students have gone home, if you use questioning regularly, you can intervene in these misunderstandings in the moment.

Find the science curriculum. Behind the

The Socratic Method

The early teacher, Socrates, developed a method of questioning that was intended to help his philosophy students reason more logically. He taught his students using a series of questions intended to help them continuously refine their thinking, deduce processes and concepts, and perform complex tasks. Socrates rehearsed the line of questioning with his students, but the young philosophers also used their teacher's dialogue method on their own to achieve learning goals they set for themselves.

In its purest form, the Socratic method involves setting a learning objective, then devising a list of questions to lead students toward the instructional goal. The questions must be designed to intrigue students, and the delivery sequence must be structured logically to lead students toward the objective in small steps. The Socratic method is the precursor of the inquiry method used to varying degrees in today's classrooms.

BUILDING YOUR CAPACITY TO QUESTION

WHAT KINDS OF QUESTIONS DO YOU ASK?

Reaping the benefits associated with skilled questioning requires awareness of different types and levels of questioning, which Part II of this minicourse examines more closely. It also requires awareness of the kinds of questions you regularly ask in your classroom. While many teachers ask questions on a frequent basis, consideration of *the kinds of questions you tend to ask most often* can help you determine an area in which you would like to build your capacity.

> While many teachers ask questions on a frequent basis, consideration of the kinds of questions you tend to ask most often can help you determine an area in which you would like to build your capacity.

For example, consider the following questions, which might be asked after students read a fictional story:

(handwritten note: does not encourage discussion)

- Who are the main characters in the story?

- What is the setting like?

- What types of things do the characters see in this setting?

- What happens to the characters in the beginning of the story?

You will likely notice right away that these questions measure students' *recall* and simple *comprehension* of the reading — and perhaps also serve to check whether they completed the assignment. While it is important to recognize that questions like these occasionally serve specific instructional goals, it is also important to note that this type of questioning does not challenge students intellectually and does not encourage discussion. These questions are like a quiz; they satisfy your need to monitor student work and their basic understanding of content.

Before teachers develop deeper questioning skills, they usually ask a greater number of this sort of question than others. While such questions *do* provide evidence that questioning is used in the classroom, they also provide important information about the *specific learning roles* questions play in that classroom. By way of comparison, consider the following questions, which could be asked after the same reading assignment:

- What kind of person do you think _____ is?

- Why do you think _____ was so important to the character?

- Why do you think the author chose this setting?

- How would the story be different if it was set in _____?
- How would you have ended this story?
- What do you think happens after the story ends?

You may observe that the questions in this second list take students' recall of the facts of the story for granted. These questions ask students to *use* factual recall in the service of higher order thinking. For example, the questions ask them to *judge*, *analyze*, *speculate*, *personalize*, and *predict*. They encourage students to *think* about the content of the story rather than merely recall it, and to engage with their peers in a consideration of the story that may lead to deeper understanding.

Advanced proficiency in questioning is not characterized by the exclusive use of any one question type. Skilled questioners employ a variety of question types for varied purposes. However, experienced teachers tend to ask a greater proportion of questions that encourage students to explore content, reflect on various points of view, and consider ideas that are new to them. They use questions to gently probe students' thinking, to seek clarification of student responses, and to challenge students intellectually.

WHO ASKS AND WHO ANSWERS QUESTIONS IN YOUR CLASSROOM?

Building capacity, then, involves first considering the range of question types you ask in your classroom as well as the relative proportion of each question type that you ask. Second, it entails reviewing who asks and who answers questions in your classroom. For example, is the exchange carefully monitored, taking place sequentially between you and another student, then you and a different student? Do students ever talk directly to one another?

As your skill with using questioning in the service of instruction advances, your goal is to become less involved in the questioning process — a notion that may seem counterintuitive. The effective use of questions in the classroom does involve honing *your* proficiency in drafting purposeful questions that motivate students to think and learn. However, an important goal of your thoughtful questions is to teach students how to engage intellectually *with each other*. Like you, they must have opportunities to rehearse these skills in the classroom. Fruitful, respectful discussion — in which students respond directly to each

Fruitful, respectful discussion — in which students respond directly to each other as you observe from the wings, facilitating only as needed — can be seen as a demonstration of advanced questioning skill.

5

other as you observe from the wings, facilitating only as needed — can be seen as a demonstration of advanced questioning skill.

HOW ENGAGED ARE YOUR STUDENTS?

A third consideration in building your capacity is students' level of engagement with the questions you currently ask in your classroom. Are students eager to answer your questions? Do all students participate? Or do the same students answer your questions time and again, while others act as spectators or are distracted? The signals students provide can indicate whether your questions are targeted to appropriate levels of cognitive difficulty, whether you are asking questions that matter to them, and whether your questions and your class climate permit and even encourage their voices to be heard.

Sensitivity to students' needs is important in establishing a questioning environment. For example, before teachers become proficient questioners, they tend primarily to ask recall questions, game-show-style — one after the other, as if a clock is ticking. "Correct" answers are provided rapid-fire by "star" students. Questions that require more advanced cognitive skill and inspire discussion, on the other hand, do not have simple right answers, and formulating responses to them takes longer. Skilled questioners give students ample time to think before asking for responses to such questions.

Also, experienced teachers seek the engagement and perspectives of all students. They facilitate this broad discussion by asking questions that ask for multiple viewpoints ("Does anyone see a different way to do this?"). They use questions to encourage students to talk to one another ("Can you ask Mary directly?"). Further, when students do not respond, proficient teachers do not provide answers to their own questions; rather, they rephrase their questions, adjust the level of difficulty, and call on students randomly.

> In a well-run discussion, everyone has a chance to speak and students listen respectfully to other students' thoughts and opinions.

The high level of student engagement that results from this sensitivity provides another marker, then, of advanced questioning skill. In a well-run discussion, everyone has a chance to speak and students listen respectfully to other students' thoughts and opinions. In addition, students are animated and appear highly interested in the questions at the heart of the discussion, and student-generated questions are permitted to move the dialogue into unplanned but serendipitous territories.

STUDENT-CENTERED FOCUS

Depending on your current level of proficiency, encouraging such a high level of student-directed activity may strike you as a loss of control over the direction of instruction. However, as you will see, with a combination of increasing skill in questioning and good management techniques, it is possible to *lead students toward* important understandings while allowing them to *arrive* at these understandings on their own.

For example, skilled teachers set the parameters for student-centered discussions by assigning reading or research prior to the class meeting, or organizing students into groups to generate ideas for the discussion in advance. Experienced facilitators use key questions (such as, "What similarities do you see among fractions, percentages, decimals, and ratios?") — or variations of that question (such as, "How is what you know about percentages linked to your understanding of fractions, decimals, or ratios?") — to originally focus the discussion and to help students continue to relate their ideas back to the purpose of the discussion. They use a series of planned questions to help students arrive at difficult concepts in stages. And they help students reason through their responses by asking for clarification ("Can you give me an example of what you mean?") and evidence ("What in our reading supports that contention?").

In leading students toward specific learning objectives, experienced teachers use student responses to generate additional questions that bring them closer and closer to the learning goal. Proficient teachers recognize the beginning of student understanding often before students do. By asking students to clarify their statements ("What do you mean by the term, _____?"), make connections ("Is that like anything else we have talked about?"), or extend their ideas to other areas ("What do you think would happen if _____?"), skilled questioners empower students to *discover* understandings targeted in advance.

> In leading students toward specific learning objectives, experienced teachers use student responses to generate additional questions that bring them closer and closer to the learning goal.

While planned questions and effective facilitation do build student understanding in a directed manner, such strategies are not designed to lead students to these understandings "by the nose." On the contrary, you *guide* student thinking with your intelligent, respectful questions. Students feel accomplishment as a result of arriving at these understandings under your direction. Such instructional techniques motivate students to think about things in ways that lead them toward achievement of your instructional goals and, ultimately, toward their own learning goals.

A LEVEL-OF-PERFORMANCE SCALE

For each of the 22 components described in *Enhancing Professional Practice: A Framework for Teaching*, there is an accompanying level-of-performance scale. The level-of-performance scale associated with the component, "Using Questioning and Discussion Techniques," is provided following this section (see Figure 1.1). The four levels of the scale — unsatisfactory, basic, proficient, and distinguished — are not intended to represent equidistant points on a continuum, nor do they represent developmental stages. Instead, they are written to describe four typical levels of performance as teachers gain experience and acquire skill in their craft. One teacher's practice for any of the components could fall over several levels. When conducting a self-assessment of your teaching practice, it is important to think in terms of what is both *current and typical*.

The "unsatisfactory" level is used to describe a performance that demonstrates little or no understanding of how questioning skill can be used to advance student learning. The "basic" performance level indicates an *understanding* of the ways questioning can be used in the service of student learning, but an inconsistent level of success in *implementing* questioning strategies. The "proficient" level represents solid, consistent use of questioning to advance student learning. And the "distinguished" level describes success in the formation of a true community of learners between the teacher and students — one in which all students are engaged with the teacher's provocative questions and in which students ask and answer questions of each other in a respectful and purposeful manner.

The four levels of performance outlined in this level-of-performance scale, and the skills described at each level, can be useful in professional dialogue about teaching, as well as for individually identifying areas in need of work and focus. The descriptions of teaching at each performance level can be used to stimulate powerful and relevant discussions of effective teaching practice among professionals.

Level-of-performance scales momentarily isolate an aspect of teaching practice in order to reflect upon it and assess your strengths, as well as areas for advancement. However, teachers who achieve a proficient level of skill in any given domain understand that, during daily practice, all components are interdependent and interwoven.

ELEMENT	UNSATISFACTORY	BASIC	PROFICIENT	DISTINGUISHED
QUALITY OF QUESTIONS	Teacher's questions are virtually all of poor quality.	Teacher's questions are a combination of low and high quality. Only some invite a response.	Most of teacher's questions are of high quality. Adequate time is available for students to respond.	Teacher's questions are of uniformly high quality, with adequate time for students to respond. Students formulate many questions.
DISCUSSION TECHNIQUES	Interaction between teacher and students is predominantly recitation style, with teacher mediating all questions and answers.	Teacher makes some attempt to engage students in a true discussion, with uneven results.	Classroom interaction represents true discussion, with teacher stepping, when appropriate, to the side.	Students assume considerable responsibility for the success of the discussion, initiating topics and making unsolicited contributions.
STUDENT PARTICIPATION	Only a few students participate in the discussion.	Teacher attempts to engage all students in the discussion, but with only limited success.	Teacher successfully engages all students in the discussion.	Students themselves ensure that all students participate in the discussion.

Figure 1.1. A Level-of-Performance Scale for Questioning and Discussion Skills
(from *Enhancing Professional Practice: A Framework for Teaching* by Charlotte Danielson).

Instead of ask "Why"
Say Help me understand—
↑ invite them to think

Christine Kathy

DOES GRADE LEVEL OR SUBJECT INFLUENCE QUESTIONING?

Questioning strategies can be applied across all grade levels and disciplines. Effective questions can be framed to help students internalize the kinds of thinking required of them by any specific discipline or by their current grade level. However, that does not mean that the *same types* of questions are appropriate for *all* disciplines and grade levels.

One of the keys to framing an effective question is targeting the level of cognitive difficulty with which students are prepared to grapple. A question that is posed well above students' ability levels can leave them feeling frustrated and incapable of learning. By the same token, a question that is too easy for them can leave them feeling bored and dissatisfied.

Building capacity to question students *in a manner that is appropriate to your subject and grade* requires understanding:

1) the *kinds* of thinking that are critical to the content area

2) the *level* of thinking students are presently capable of doing

Students' current thinking skills indicate how you must frame your questions today, while the thinking skills valued by your subject area point toward your cognitive goals for your students. Your skillful questions can be used to help students achieve those goals over time.

A full discussion of questioning strategies by subject and age level is beyond the scope of this workbook. However, in recognition of the importance of these issues to your practice, Appendix B provides a list of additional resources by grade and subject.[5] In Related Activities at the end of Part I, you are asked to read one of these articles or another of your own choosing, and to subsequently reflect on subject and grade-level considerations that matter to you.

As you may imagine, the fact that questions are targeted at specific ability levels also has important consequences for multi-ability classrooms — a topic that is addressed in Part III. For this reason, articles on questioning and discussion involving children with special needs are also included in Appendix B.

> *One of the keys to framing an effective question is targeting the level of cognitive difficulty with which students are prepared to grapple.*

[5]This resource list is intended as a starting place for teachers' efforts to locate articles on questioning that are appropriate to their individual practices. However, educators using the minicourse are responsible for previewing and selecting materials that best meet the needs of their schools and communities. Presentation of these resources does not represent endorsement by Educational Testing Service of the points of view represented in the articles.

Other findings from research:

* Questions during a lesson provides
better quality than instruction without
the ~~those~~ questions embedded.

* Oral questions during instruction
are more effective than written questions.

* On average 60% of questions lower level questions
20% higher level questions.
20% procedural (did you do your homework)

* Increasing the use of higher level questions
produces higher gains.

Directions: The following activities are intended to help you identify areas for growth in understanding the value and effective use of questioning and discussion skills. The activities should be completed sequentially and in a manner conducive to your own individual learning style.

	COMPLETED
1 Review one or two articles that address questioning and discussion techniques within the context of your subject and/or instructional grade level. The resource list provided in Appendix B can help you locate an article for this activity. Alternatively, you may find one online, in the library, or in a professional journal.	
2 Using **My Minicourse Journal**, which follows, reflect on the article(s) you read and assess your current teaching practice. Questions are provided to guide your reflection.	
3 What would you like to be able to say about your questioning skills at some point in the future? In the **My Goals for Questioning Skills** chart, which follows, list three to five measurable claims you would like to be able to make in the column labeled *Goals*, and suggest two to four steps you can take toward your goals in the column labeled *Activities*.	

	COMPLETED
4 If you wish, discuss this topic with other teachers. Take notes during the discussion in the **What I Learned From Other Teachers** chart, which follows, to help you recall what was said. If you are a member of a study group, you may want to suggest using activity 1, above, as a study topic. The following question may help start a professional conversation: ■ How does the use of questioning as an instructional strategy vary by subject or grade level?	
5 Plan to visit the classroom of a teacher who is experienced and proficient in using questioning and discussion skills with students. As you watch this teacher's lesson, take notes in the **Classroom Visit** chart, which follows. Questions are provided to guide your reflections on the visit.	

my minicourse
Journal

1. *How does what you read compare with your own professional experiences?*

2. *Which subject- or grade-specific thinking skills do you think questioning and/or discussion techniques may help you promote?*

3. *How do subject or grade-level considerations influence the way questioning and/or discussion techniques should be used in your classroom?*

4. Refer to the level-of-performance scale provided in Part I (Figure 1.1). How would you rate your current proficiency in using questioning and discussion techniques? What are your strengths? In what areas do you most want to improve?

* Quality. law and high due to age young. But very good at giving wait time

* Basic due to age- we work on turn taking non verbal and conversational exchange w/ various cues.

* Will engage my students in discussion with various cues/ structure.

5. How ready are your students to respond to a new level of questioning or to generate/refine their own questions? How do you know?

GOALS	ACTIVITIES
Example: *I would like to be able to develop questions that really make my students think.*	Example: *1. Learn which question types promote student thinking.* *2. Learn strategies for supporting and guiding student responses.* *3. Increase opportunities for discussion.* *4. Listen better.*
1	
2	
3	
4	
5	

What I Learned From Other Teachers	
TEACHER	INPUT

Classroom Visit

DATE: _____ CLASSROOM TEACHER'S NAME: _____ LESSON CONTENT: _____

QUESTIONS TO GUIDE YOUR REFLECTIONS ON THE CLASSROOM VISIT:

■ What did you notice about the wording and cognitive level of the teacher's questions?

■ How much time did students spend actively engaged in discussion?

■ How would you describe students' level of engagement?

■ What evidence of student learning did you see?

■ What did the teacher do to help students feel comfortable sharing their ideas?

■ What did the teacher do to encourage students to lengthen or clarify their responses?

■ What have you learned from watching this experienced professional at work?

■ What techniques and strategies can you take from this classroom visit for use in your classroom?

Notes:

PART II

A VARIETY OF QUESTION TYPES

While the use of questions to drive instruction may be a pervasive teaching practice, not all questions produce the same results. Some questions, such as those that require recitation ("Who was the first president of the United States?"), ask students to recall a specific parcel of knowledge and require no further engagement. On the other hand, other questions ("Why do you think George Washington was chosen to be the first president of the United States?") ask students to evaluate or analyze information for a specific purpose and may require research or other forms of inquiry.

There are many ways of looking at question types. Some typologies define question types using multiple categories. For example, one popular way to distinguish questions relies on Bloom's taxonomy of the six cognitive levels on which particular questions draw. Another organizational structure looks at the various thinking tasks that different kinds of questions require students to perform — such as *recalling* or *predicting* — while another categorizes questions according to teachers' purposes — such as questions teachers use to manage independent or group work, facilitate discussion, or probe students' responses. Still another organizer focuses on questions that require students to reflect on ways they think and learn.

Questions are also sometimes viewed using schemes that break them into only two types — such as high and low, or open and closed. These binary typologies can be used in conjunction with other hierarchies to add a second dimension of skill.

An understanding of question types can help you reflect on the range of questions you use in your classroom and can help you plan specific ways to improve your questioning skill. Part II of this minicourse presents several ways of looking at question types, as well as the purposes for which different question types are best used; example questions are provided for each type. Next, Part II explores the dynamics of using a variety of question types in the classroom. Related Activities in this section are designed to help you evaluate the range of questions types you typically use in your classroom and to reflect on question types you would like to try in Part IV.

As you review the question types presented in Part II, you will likely find that the organizational structures overlap. They are not intended to be mutually exclusive. It may be helpful to you to think of these classification schemes as many sides of the same question "jewel." As you hold the universe of questions in your hand and view it from side to side, these devices are intended to shed light on a particular facet of the beauty of questions, rather than to define questions anew. Thus, from one side of the jewel you may see several others.

Also, the lists of question types presented here — while intended to represent a *variety* of ways of looking at question types — do not represent *all* ways of viewing questions. As you review the lists, it may be helpful to add to the lists, or to note your ideas about the strengths and weaknesses of each approach in the margins of the workbook. In the end, you may settle on your own way of organizing questions.

Depending on your professional experiences, one way of looking at question types may be more useful to you than others. It is not necessary for you to be able to categorize the questions you ask in your classroom according to these or any structure. These organizers are merely aids for your thinking and planning. One or more of these organizational approaches may be useful to you when reflecting on the range of questions you use in your classroom and planning ways to improve your questioning skills.

BLOOM'S TAXONOMY OF COGNITIVE SKILLS

Bloom's taxonomy can be helpful in drafting questions intended to achieve particular cognitive goals.

As you know, Bloom's taxonomy[6] orders cognitive skills from low to high, with simple recall of knowledge at the low end of the scale and more elaborate thinking processes, such as evaluation skill, at the high end. Bloom's taxonomy can be helpful in drafting questions intended to achieve particular cognitive goals. The chart on the following pages briefly describes each of the levels of Bloom's taxonomy and provides examples of questions meant to elicit the type of thinking described at each level.

[6]Benjamin Bloom (Ed.). (1956). *Taxonomy of educational objectives. Handbook 1: Cognitive domain.* New York: David McKay.

KNOWLEDGE —

REQUIRES STUDENTS TO RECALL LEARNED INFORMATION, SUCH AS FACTS, CONCEPTS, DEFINITIONS, AND FORMULAS. FOR EXAMPLE:

- Who was the 16th President of the United States?

- What is the correct order of operations for equations?

- What is an adjective?

COMPREHENSION —

REQUIRES STUDENTS TO DEMONSTRATE UNDERSTANDING OF LEARNED INFORMATION, SUCH AS BY PRODUCING EXPLANATIONS OR PROVIDING EXAMPLES. FOR INSTANCE:

- What was one of President Lincoln's contributions to American history?

- What could happen if you did not follow the correct order of operations for equations?

- What are some examples of adjectives?

APPLICATION —

REQUIRES STUDENTS TO USE LEARNED INFORMATION — SUCH AS RULES, FORMULAS, CONCEPTS, AND PROCEDURES — IN NEW SITUATIONS, SUCH AS TO SOLVE A PROBLEM OR PERFORM A NEW TASK.

- What problems related to slavery was Lincoln unable to solve?

- Using the order of operations rule, how would you solve the problem on page 9?

- What adjectives would you use to describe your bedroom?

[handwritten notes in margin:]
What did Ivan feed the flower?
Does pizza help a flower grow?
Determine is an application question
What happened outside.

ANALYSIS —

REQUIRES STUDENTS TO BREAK SOMETHING DOWN AND EXPLAIN ITS COMPONENT PARTS AS WELL AS THE RELATIONSHIPS BETWEEN THOSE COMPONENTS.

- How did events in the first half of the nineteenth century lead to the Civil War?

- What steps would you have to take to solve the word problem on page 22?

- How do the adjectives the author uses ultimately reveal her point of view?

SYNTHESIS —

REQUIRES STUDENTS TO JOIN COMPONENTS IN ORDER TO CREATE A NEW WHOLE.

- How might you use strategies similar to Lincoln's to compose a contemporary memorial address?

- Keeping the order of operations rule in mind, how would you write an equation to solve the problem?

- Can you write a descriptive paragraph that demonstrates your understanding of adjectives?

EVALUATION —

REQUIRES STUDENTS TO USE SPECIFIC CRITERIA TO MAKE AN ASSESSMENT.

- Using the rubric we discussed, what score would you give the Gettysburg Address?

- Knowing that I gave an answer of 19 for the problem, can you determine how I incorrectly applied the order of operations rule?

- How is *The Last of the Mohicans* characteristic or not characteristic of nineteenth-century American literature?

Questions That Direct Thinking Tasks

Another way of looking at the kind of thinking that questions require of students is to focus on the *task* — rather than the cognitive process — that a specific question asks students to perform. Thinking of questions this way can help you focus on *what you want students to do* in response to the question. Focusing on thinking tasks can guide you in choosing language for your questions that specifies the intended task. The chart that follows briefly describes some thinking tasks students are typically asked to perform and provides examples of questions that are worded to elicit those thinking tasks.

> *Focusing on thinking tasks can guide you in choosing language for your questions that specifies the intended task.*

Thinking Task Questions

Observe —

Requires students to provide detail about what they noticed or saw.

- What did you notice about the main character?

- What did you see when you examined the flower?

- How did the candidates use body language in their speeches?

Recall —

Requires students to recite previously learned information.

- What do you recall about the main character from your reading?

- What do you remember about photosynthesis?

- What issues were important to taxpayers during this election?

COMPARE —
REQUIRES STUDENTS TO FIND SIMILARITIES AMONG ITEMS.

- What is similar about the two main characters?

- How are these two plants alike?

- How were the candidates' platforms alike?

CONTRAST —
REQUIRES STUDENTS TO FIND DIFFERENCES AMONG ITEMS.

- What is different about the two main characters?

- How are these two plants different?

- How were the candidates' speeches different?

CLASSIFY —
REQUIRES STUDENTS TO GROUP ITEMS BASED ON THEIR SIMILARITIES.

- How would you categorize the two main characters?

- Where in the classification scheme do these two plants belong?

- How would you describe the candidate's position?

PREDICT —
REQUIRES STUDENTS TO MAKE PREDICTIONS BASED ON THEIR UNDERSTANDING.

- What do you think is going to happen to the characters next?

- What do you think will happen if you deprive the plant of light?

- What do you think will be important to voters in our election?

SPECULATE —
REQUIRES STUDENTS TO IMAGINE BEYOND WHAT
THEY KNOW.

- What kind of characters would you create for this story?

- Can you imagine a plant with other useful qualities?

- Can you imagine yourself one day running for political office?

DEMONSTRATE —
REQUIRES STUDENTS TO DEMONSTRATE A SKILL OR CONCEPT
FOR OTHERS.

- Can the three of you enact the scene for the class?

- How could you demonstrate this process in the science fair?

- Can you show us how a candidate could use body language effectively?

EVALUATE —
REQUIRES STUDENTS TO EXAMINE AND EVALUATE A
PERFORMANCE.

- How did the students' enactment make you think differently about the scene?

- What do the results of your experiment say about photosynthesis?

- How could you strengthen your campaign?

MANAGING STUDENTS AS THEY WORK

Questions can also be grouped according to teachers' purposes by looking at the behaviors they are intended to elicit from students. Such questions can help you manage independent or group work, facilitate discussion, or probe students' responses. The list that follows briefly describes some of these kinds of questions and provides examples of them as well.

MANAGEMENT QUESTIONS

MANAGE —

HELPS YOU GET STUDENTS ORGANIZED FOR A GROUP TASK.

- What direction did you agree on?

- Is someone in the group taking notes?

- How have you divided responsibilities?

CLARIFY —

HELPS YOU UNDERSTAND STUDENTS' RESPONSES IN ORDER TO KNOW HOW TO HELP THEM.

- What steps did you use to get that answer?

- Can you explain what you mean by '____?'

- Can you give me an example of what you mean?

ORIENT —

HELPS YOU FOCUS STUDENTS' THINKING FOR AN INTENDED PURPOSE.

- What specifically does the project ask you to do?

- What are the key words in the question?

- How can you find that information?

REFOCUS —
HELPS YOU REDIRECT STUDENTS' EFFORTS ON A TASK.

- How does your example relate to the question?

- Can you think of other ways to reach your goal?

- That's an example of _____; can you give an example of _____ instead?

MONITOR —
HELPS YOU CHECK STUDENTS' PROGRESS OR ENGAGEMENT.

- Does everyone have something to do?

- Has everyone completed part 1 of the assignment?

- Does anyone need more time?

PROBE —
HELPS YOU CHALLENGE STUDENTS TO THINK MORE DEEPLY, CONSTRUCT MEANING, OR UNCOVER RELATIONSHIPS.

- What does that suggest to you?

- Have you ever seen something like this before?

- What would happen if you reversed it?

EXTEND —
HELPS YOU INVOLVE MORE STUDENTS AND EXPAND THE FOCUS OF DISCUSSION FROM THE SPECIFIC TO THE GENERAL.

- Can anyone suggest another possibility?

- What could the phenomenon that _____ mentioned represent?

- Do you see any repetition of this idea elsewhere?

NARROW —

HELPS YOU SHIFT THE FOCUS OF DISCUSSION FROM THE GENERAL TO THE SPECIFIC.

- What do these things suggest about the process that is involved here?

- What do your examples tell you about the author's point of view?

- What are we leaving out of this discussion?

SUMMARIZE —

HELPS YOU CONCLUDE A DISCUSSION OR SEGUE INTO A NEW TASK BY ASKING STUDENTS TO ENCAPSULATE THE MAIN POINTS.

- Can you say what you learned in your own words?

- Can we list the main issues the class identified?

- What conclusions have we reached?

LOW-LEVEL AND HIGH-LEVEL QUESTIONS

> *Low-level questions are those that require students to respond using relatively straightforward thought processes, while high-level questions demand integrated critical thinking.*

As noted earlier, it is possible to group question types into categories such as "low" and "high." Low-level questions are those that require students to respond using relatively straightforward thought processes, while high-level questions demand integrated critical thinking.

"Low" and "high" can be used to divide more complex taxonomies into subcategories. For example, in Bloom's taxonomy, knowledge, comprehension, and application questions could be considered low-level, and questions that require analysis, synthesis, and evaluation could be considered high-level. This can help you gauge whether the variety of questions you ask falls at one end of the spectrum or the other.

Both low-level and high-level questions have their place in the classroom. For example, when you wish to determine that students grasp basic content before they undertake a more challenging project, you would use low-level questions. On the other hand, to elicit deeper thinking from students, you would ask high-level questions.

LOW-LEVEL QUESTIONS ARE OFTEN USED TO:

- determine how well students are prepared for a task

- diagnose gaps in students' knowledge

- summarize information students will use to perform a task

HIGH-LEVEL QUESTIONS ARE OFTEN USED TO:

- help students find solutions to complex problems

- drive a discussion to a deeper level

- encourage students to think in new ways

It is important to keep in mind that what constitutes a low-level question for one student may pose a high-level challenge for another. For example, the multiplication problem posed by the question, "What is 9 x 3?" is a matter of simple recall for the student who is accomplished at math facts and now uses multiplication to perform higher-order operations. However, the same math question may require significant problem solving and encourage much thoughtful exploration for the student who is learning to multiply for the first time.

OPEN AND CLOSED QUESTIONS

Another useful way to think of question types is to distinguish between open and closed questions. Unlike high-level and low-level questions, open and closed questions do not suggest the level of thinking that is required to answer them. Rather, they refer to the range of possible responses.

An **open question** has many possible answers. You may not always be able to anticipate student responses to these questions, but you can still judge their quality. For example, the question, "How would you solve the problem?" allows students the freedom to make a wide range of choices, but how well students apply their skills in doing so determines the quality of their responses.

A **closed question**, on the other hand, has a specific number of possible answers. For example, there is only one correct answer to the question, "What is the formula for computing speed?" Similarly, there are a limited number of correct answers to the question, "Can you name three planets in our solar system?" You usually know the answers to closed questions before students answer them, and you can easily judge a correct response from an incorrect one.

Many teachers express a preference for open-ended questions because they believe they encourage students to think. However, being open-ended does not, by itself, make a question meaningful to students. It is important to understand that both open questions and closed questions can elicit student thinking at low and high levels.

For instance, the open question, "What natural resources do you use at home?" and the closed question, "What is the definition of a natural resource?" are both low-level questions. Similarly, the open question, "What are some ways these countries might resolve their conflict?" and the closed question, "Considering the data you have recorded, would you say the process is aerobic or anaerobic?" both require students to perform complex evaluations.

Both open and closed questions, then, play a role in student learning. When planning questions, it is important to consider the cognitive level or task the question prompts as well as whether it is open or closed.

It is important to understand that both open questions and closed questions can elicit student thinking at low and high levels.

THINKING ABOUT THINKING

Metacognitive questions encourage students to reflect on their own thinking processes. Such questions can help make students more aware of the ways in which they learn, reach conclusions, and evaluate people and circumstances. The goal of metacognitive questions is to help students refine their thinking and gain better control over their learning. When asked questions that prompt them to do this, students rehearse important discovery processes they can also employ on their own. The list that follows describes some metacognitive thinking tasks and provides examples of questions intended to elicit each type of thinking.

> The goal of metacognitive questions is to help students refine their thinking and gain better control over their learning.

METACOGNITIVE QUESTIONS

REFLECT —
ENCOURAGES STUDENTS TO THINK ABOUT THE CHOICES THEY MAKE AND THEIR REASONS FOR THEM.

- How did you try to solve the problem?

- Why did you choose that approach?

- What additional approaches can you try?

- What made you link _____ with _____?

PERSONALIZE —
ENCOURAGES STUDENTS TO INTERNALIZE IDEAS OR EMPATHIZE WITH OTHERS.

- How would you feel if it happened to you or someone you know?

- How would you teach the process to another student?

- Do you have any personal experiences with _____?

- How would you react if a character in a movie did that?

VERIFY —
ENCOURAGES STUDENTS TO REFLECT ON THE VERACITY OF INFORMATION ON WHICH THEY BASE THEIR IDEAS.

- What made you decide that this was an example of the process?

- What in the reading supports your theory?

- What personal experiences or other evidence led you to that conclusion?

- Have you checked to make sure that what you were told is true?

QUESTION —
ENCOURAGES STUDENTS TO REFLECT ON QUESTIONS AND TO APPROACH IDEAS WITH SKEPTICISM.

- Why do you suppose _____ asked that question?

- Do you think the process *always* applies?

- What might motivate the author to argue for this point?

- What questions that are *not* asked might be interesting to ask?

IDEALIZE —
ENCOURAGES STUDENTS TO VISUALIZE GOALS THAT WILL DIRECT THEIR EFFORTS.

- How will you feel when you are ready?

- What do you want it to look like when you are finished?

- Are there any real world examples you can use as models?

- How will you know you are successful?

REVISE —

ENCOURAGES STUDENTS TO EVALUATE THEIR WORK IN ORDER
TO IMPROVE IT.

- Which parts do you want to strengthen?

- Where do you need help?

- What would you do differently next time?

- What do you need in order to do that?

UTILIZE —

ENCOURAGES STUDENTS TO CONSIDER RESOURCES THAT CAN
HELP THEM REACH THEIR GOALS.

- Are there any guidelines you can use?

- Who can you ask about this?

- Where can you learn that information?

- What do you already know that can help you?

APPLYING DIFFERENT QUESTION TYPES

It is important to bear in mind that all question types are important in the classroom. Placing questions in hierarchies suggests that we value processes at the high end of the scale more than we do those at the lower end. And indeed we may! But, in fact, students cannot develop higher-order thinking processes without first mastering lower-order thinking skills. Thus, low-level questions have value in developing student capacities to think and learn.

In other words, all levels of thinking, and therefore the question types that elicit them, are interdependent. Your skill is in knowing which questions are appropriate for your students *when*, and in using your questions to challenge your students to pursue deeper and deeper levels of thinking. To respond effectively to students' changing needs, you must be prepared, even within the course of a discussion or lesson, to vary your use of question types.

> To respond effectively to students' changing needs, you must be prepared, even within the course of a discussion or lesson, to vary your use of question types.

There are several very good reasons to vary the question types you use in your daily teaching practice. First, research[7] shows that teachers who employ a variety of question types — that is, questions that target low-level thinking skills *and* those that target high-level thinking skills — are more likely to increase student learning than teachers who use only questions targeted at low-level thinking skills. Furthermore, by increasing the proportion of high-level questions they use, teachers can boost student achievement.

Second, as we have seen, question types are as varied as your goals for student learning. Just as one type of skill does not make a well-rounded student, one type of question cannot help you develop all student skills. For example, recitation questions may demonstrate that students have learned important information, but questions on this level do not reflect students' problem solving ability. Only questions that ask students to think more deeply — to simultaneously recall information, apply it, and evaluate the consequences, for instance — elicit high-order thinking.

Third, there *is* a spontaneous factor to using questions. Like any plans you prepare for your classes, when you are implementing planned questions, you must be sensitive to your students' abilities to respond to them. For example, a lack of response from students may indicate that you are asking "too much too soon" — a signal to rephrase the question or to ask a lower-level question.

[7]Cotton, K. Classroom questioning. Northwest Regional Educational Laboratory: School Improvement Research Series. Available: http://www.nwrel.org/scpd/3/cu5.html.

Similarly, if students seem distracted instead of challenged by your questions, they may be ready for higher-level questions. Knowing what to ask and when to ask it *is* a matter of planning, but it also requires sensitivity and flexibility.

Fourth, just as sensitivity to students' readiness for specific questions can help you determine what to ask when, listening to students' responses to questions can help you know what to ask *next*. Students' responses reveal their thinking processes and suggest where they may be capable of going next. Your well-timed question can take them there.

It may be useful to think of this instructional strategy of varying question types as *scaffolding* student learning. By using your awareness of students' thinking to guide your questioning, you provide a support system that can help your students climb to new levels.

MANAGING DISCUSSION

The natural result of posing appealing, challenging, and purposeful questions in your classroom is discussion, which may be thought of as a collaborative response to your queries. Early — and most likely partial — student responses to your key question stimulate other students' thinking, which leads to deeper responses and, ultimately, to an exchange of ideas among students. Initially, your students may require a series of questions from you to fuel discussion. But as your skill and comfort — and your students' skill and comfort — with questioning advance, students begin to internalize questioning and listening attitudes. Then their responses, as well as the questions they form, begin to drive discussion.

The beauty of discussion is that, like other forms of teamwork, each individual benefits from the collective efforts of the group.

The beauty of discussion is that, like other forms of teamwork, each individual benefits from the collective efforts of the group. A good discussion is like a window into a large, complex mind shared by your students. Each student's contribution has the power to shift the thinking of the group in a new direction. Each student has the potential to be awakened by thoughts that individual habits of mind, personal biases, and experiences may have otherwise constrained. By listening to others, a struggling student may learn new ways of connecting ideas or solving problems. A factual problem solver may think for the first time about obstacles that must be considered if the solution is to be meaningful for everyone. In the end, the answers to the questions you pose are richer, fuller, and wider as a result of discussion.

In addition to enriching and extending students' thinking, productive discussion also teaches students social skills that are important in a democratic society. For example, they can learn to listen and respond respectfully when they encounter unfamiliar ideas — ideas that may be based on personal, social, or cultural differences among students. Culturally sheltered students may begin to understand what it means to grow up in circumstances different from their own. In a sea of superficial differences, students may find connections with others they did not imagine existed. Students may or may not learn acceptance of their differences over time, but they may at least learn that — whether or not they agree with all students on issues of some importance — they can work together as a community with diverse individuals.

Discussion provides a venue for students to develop, refine, reflect upon, and monitor their own thinking. Students who are hesitant to respond, for example, may hear other students successfully express their thoughts and begin to see how they may voice theirs. After discussion has ended, students may continue to consider how they expressed themselves and how they may do so more satisfyingly next time. What's more, after listening to others, students may continue to reflect on ideas they heard and the origins of their own ideas, ultimately aligning their thinking more and more with their own ideas of who they are and want to be.

Discussion provides a venue for students to develop, refine, reflect upon, and monitor their own thinking.

The ability of your students to engage in productive discussion depends in part on your comfort and skill in posing question types to suit a variety of purposes, as well as questions that motivate and challenge student thinking. In addition, as Part III of this minicourse details further, your flexibility, your ability to think on your feet, and your sensitivity to your students also influence success with discussion. It is important to remember that both you and your students can develop or improve these skills incrementally. Part III suggests ways to build your students' capacities for discussion as you advance your own skill with questioning students and facilitating discussion.

STUDENT-GENERATED QUESTIONS

Student-generated questions can be a powerful tool in creating relevance for students. When student-generated questions determine the direction and tenor of discussion, you can be certain that students are interested in what's being said. When students formulate their own questions, and have a role in how they will answer them, they are engaged at the highest level possible.

> When students formulate their own questions, and have a role in how they will answer them, they are engaged at the highest level possible.

Teachers who use student-generated questions to enrich instruction share responsibility for learning with students. When students' questions are given a place of importance in the classroom, students learn to use their questions to guide their independent learning. If students respond only to teacher questions, they are still essentially followers on the learning path. When they are permitted to lead with their own questions, they gain confidence in their own thinking and become motivated to seek their own answers.

As you build your questioning and discussion skills, you will likely see benefits to using student-generated questions to enrich instructional conversation. The first benefit may be students' positive responses to your use of their questions. Students feel great pride in asking "a good question" — perhaps as much as in giving a "good answer." This level of interest and respect students show when their questions are used to fuel class discussion may alone justify using them.

In addition, teacher questions and student questions contribute differently to student learning. A recent study reported that, while teacher-directed discussions were found to be more effective in achieving higher levels of reasoning with students, student-led discussions were more generative and exploratory.[8] As both high levels of reasoning *and* the generation and exploration of ideas are important to student learning, using a mixture of teacher-generated and student-generated questions may be most desirable for your discussions.

One way to accomplish this is to ask students to write two or three questions as they prepare for a lesson. After reviewing these, you can choose a few to use in your planned discussion. For example, you could intersperse a few student questions in a systematic and fair manner at appropriate moments during discussion, or you could reserve a period of time exclusively for student questions. If a student question can be used as a substitute for one of your own, increased student engagement would argue strongly for the switch.

← Then go back and answer.

If you're asking good questions — They will ask good questions

Student-generated questions have the power to reveal much about student learning. For example, a student question can bring to light an obstacle to understanding. By the same token, a student question can point you to new ways of looking at your subject matter. Student questions indicate what students find important and what interests them. Your willingness to allow student questions to influence discussion can make students more willing to embrace ideas other than their own. What's more, your increased understanding of student thinking can help you teach them more effectively.

> *Student questions indicate what students find important and what interests them.*

Of course, it takes time to create a student-centered learning environment in which group discussion, enriched

---

[8]Hogan, K., Nastasi, B. K., Pressley, M. (1999). Discourse patterns and collaborative scientific reasoning in peer and teacher-guided discussions. *Cognition & Instruction, 17*(4), 379-432.

with student questions, flourishes. Your students' capacity to question advances with your questioning skill. First, as you ask your students more varied and purposeful questions, and they become more comfortable responding to them, students take the first step toward learning to question — understanding the value of a good question. The clearer and more precise your questioning language — which is discussed further in Part IV — the more likely it is that students will see specific purposes of questions. (Initially, you may even hear yourself — your questioning style and language — mirrored in their questions.) Next, your metacognitive questions encourage students to consider the type of thinking that particular kinds of questions require of them. Finally, structured practice and class discussion of supporting attitudes for successful student questioning — discussed in more depth in Part III — build students' confidence in their ability to question and increase their willingness to voice questions.

THINKING ABOUT QUESTIONS

In order to formulate their own questions, students must have some awareness of the type of thinking that particular kinds of questions require of them. They must understand the nature and function of the question types *you ask of them*, and they must be shown how to use this information to target *their* questions to your requirements.

For these reasons, you may sometimes wish to take a structured approach to reflecting on questioning strategies with your students. While some students may be natural questioners, others benefit from reflecting on, analyzing, and categorizing question types. In either case, students' abilities to respond to your questions and to draft their own questions improve with this kind of practice and reflection.

> While some students may be natural questioners, others benefit from reflecting on, analyzing, and categorizing question types.

You can use metacognitive questions (such as, "What questions that are not asked might be interesting to ask?") to prepare students to ask their own questions, as well as to encourage students to reflect on ways they engage intellectually with ideas ("What made you link _____ with _____?"). For these reasons, you may wish to make a separate effort to incorporate metacognitive questions into your discussion. While there will be times when you use metacognitive questions as an appropriate tool to help students formulate responses to content questions (e.g., "Can you explain for us how you arrived at that idea?"), or to generate questions, they may be used at other times solely to encourage students to reflect on how they learn.

Related Activities for Students, at the end of Part III, suggest ways you can encourage students to reflect on how they think and learn, as well as ways you can prepare students for responding to and asking questions.

Directions: The following activities are intended to help you explore your use of question types for different instructional purposes. The activities should be completed sequentially and in a manner conducive to your own individual learning style.

		COMPLETED
1	Review any or all of the taxonomies of question types provided in Part II (or another taxonomy of your own choosing). In **My Minicourse Journal**, which follows, reflect on the types of questions you ask in your classroom. Questions are provided to guide your reflection.	
2	Consider the questioning skills you wish to improve and the goals you identified in Part I in the **My Goals for Questioning Skills** chart. In the **My New Questions** chart, which follows, consider opportunities your classes present for using questions to advance these goals. Note examples of questions that you could use with your students to achieve specific learning goals and enhance their learning. (Try some question types you don't typically use.) Don't worry too much about the wording of your questions now. In Part IV, when you plan a lesson supported by questions, you will be able to refine them.	

3 Consider the taxonomies of question types provided earlier in this section. Do they suit your needs? Use the **My Own Taxonomy** chart, which follows, to describe question types you feel are important but have not been described. Provide examples of these question types.

4 If you wish, discuss your thoughts with other teachers. Take notes during the discussion in the **What I Learned From Other Teachers** chart, which follows, to help you recall what was said. If you are a member of a study group, you may want to suggest completing activity 3 together. The following question may help start a professional conversation:

■ Are certain question types particularly well suited to specific disciplines or grade levels? Why or why not?

my minicourse
Journal

1. *With which question types are you most comfortable and proficient?*

2. *With which question types are your students most comfortable and proficient? How can you tell?*

3. *Which question types would you like to become more proficient in using? Why?*

4. *What is the "next level" of questioning that is right for your students? How do you know?*

5. *What kind of skill development will your students need to reach this "next level" of questioning?*

INSTRUCTIONAL OPPORTUNITY	QUESTION TYPE/LEVEL	POSSIBLE QUESTIONS
Examples: 1) Historical understanding of *The Scarlet Letter*. 2) Understanding of the similarities and differences among percentages, fractions, decimals, and ratios.	Examples: 1) evaluation, high-level, open 2) evaluation, high-level, open	Examples: 1) "What does the red letter 'A' worn by Hester Prynne in *The Scarlet Letter* tell us about seventeenth-century morality?" 2) "How is what you know about percentages linked to your understanding of fractions, decimals, or ratios?"

My Own Taxonomy

Question Type	Description	Example Questions

What I Learned From Other Teachers	
TEACHER	INPUT

PART III

OBJECTIVES:

- UNDERSTAND HOW CLASS CLIMATE AND INTERPERSONAL SKILLS IMPACT STUDENT RESPONSES.

- CONSIDER WAYS TO ENCOURAGE STUDENTS TO RESPOND TO QUESTIONS.

- CONSIDER WAYS TO PREPARE STUDENTS FOR NEW QUESTIONING STRATEGIES.

- REFLECT ON INDIVIDUAL INTERPERSONAL SKILLS, CLASS CLIMATE, AND POTENTIAL OBSTACLES TO QUESTIONING.

ENCOURAGING STUDENT RESPONSES

In order for your authentic questions to prompt genuine, thoughtful student responses and fruitful student discussions, it is important to consider the interpersonal skills and classroom climate that foster such exchanges. An understanding of the climate and attitudes that support purposeful questioning and discussion can help you earn your students' trust, encourage student responses, and help students see how this process benefits them.

In questioning students, you ask them to take a personal risk. *Tell me what goes on inside your mind*, your questions ask. *Share with the class and me some thoughts you may never have shared with others*. In exchange, you promise students that their ideas will be treated seriously and respectfully; that you will support both their responses and the questions they ask; and that the process of questioning will benefit them in important ways.

Productive classroom discussion hinges on this subtle pact between you and students and a similar one between each student and the rest of the class. But how do you arrive at such an agreement with students? How do *you* gain their trust? What do *you* need to know to fulfill your part of the bargain?

Part III of this minicourse examines specific interpersonal skills and aspects of classroom environment that encourage students to open up to questions and discussion. Two sets of Related Activities are provided at the end of Part III. Related Activities for the Teacher can help you reflect on your current communication skills and your classroom environment, visualize the skills and environment you would like to achieve, and begin considering potential obstacles to advancing your level of questioning. Use Related Activities for Students to help accustom your students to a questioning environment.

As you consider classroom attitudes and climate in Part III, it may be helpful to remember that the process of maintaining positive attitudes and a supportive classroom environment is actually a very dynamic one. Managing this aspect of your practice successfully depends on your willingness to be flexible, to listen, and to think on your feet. If you are new to questioning, you may feel a little overwhelmed at first by all there is to think about. But as with any new skill, you can start by mastering a few simple steps. Don't worry if your movements feel a little mechanical at first. Later, as the steps become more natural, you will find yourself putting them together in new and exciting ways.

INITIAL PREPARATION FOR QUESTIONING

Before implementing a questioning strategy, you may want to consider a few preliminary steps you can take regarding your knowledge of your students and the physical attributes of your classroom. By considering these issues ahead of time, you may be able to prevent some common obstacles to successful questioning.

STUDENT NAMES

The interpersonal exchanges that take place during questioning and discussion require that you know all of your students by name. On a personal level, it is very important to students that you know who they are by name; it tells them you see them as individuals. While this sign of respect is itself important to encouraging student responses, in class discussion names are also important as a management tool. In your conversations with students, you will have to address them directly, and in the course of discussion, you will frequently refer to students' previous responses using speakers' names. If you don't already know your students by name, create a seating chart and learn them before you start.

PHYSICAL ENVIRONMENT

The physical classroom environment can impact the success of your class discussions. For example, teachers and students cannot talk comfortably with one another in a large space in which students sit at some distance from the teacher. You and your students should not have to struggle to hear one another, and students should not have to turn to see each other. Consider the physical attributes of your classroom. Can students hear you easily? Is the seating conducive to communication among students? If it is possible, given the limits of space and the size of your class, you may want to rearrange student seating for the purposes of discussion. A circle is most effective for this purpose, but if you do not have room, you might wish to have all students turn their seats toward the center of the room to maximize their ability to face each other.

PERSONAL CIRCUMSTANCES

It may be wise to reflect on your knowledge of students' personal circumstances before you pursue deeper questioning with them. During lectures, students learn at an impersonal distance from subject matter, but during discussion, content can affect them in ways that are very personal. For instance, asking a student with learning difficulties a math question that is too difficult can leave him/her feeling incompetent and embarrassed — especially if others answer it easily. Similarly, a discussion about a literary character who dies can be hard on a student who recently lost a family member. By making efforts to stay aware of your students' personal circumstances, you can avoid these potentially painful questioning experiences.

A Note About Students With Learning Challenges

Questioning can pose difficulties for students with learning challenges. When questioning students with special needs, it may be helpful to consult with the child's resource teacher to determine appropriate questions. S/he may recommend that you give the student the question in advance, be sure you have the student's attention before asking the question, allow more wait time for a response, and be ready to rephrase or repeat the question at the student's request.

CALLING ON STUDENTS

Before beginning a new questioning approach, it is also useful to consider how you will call on students to speak. During discussion, it is easy to lose track of who you have called on and who has not yet spoken. It makes sense to decide in advance on a fair method that makes this easier for you and that students understand. Remember that one of your goals is to maximize participation by drawing in students who may not normally speak up.

One point to consider is whether to call on volunteers or nonvolunteers. While calling on volunteers may be less threatening to students who are unaccustomed to speaking up in class, this practice tends to encourage only strong speakers to participate. Among the students who are not speaking may be quiet students who *want* to speak but do not know how to insert

> Remember that one of your goals is to maximize participation by drawing in students who may not normally speak up.

themselves in the conversation. By calling on nonvolunteers, you can actually provide the help they need to voice their thoughts.

On the other hand, once a discussion gets rolling, it can be very frustrating for students who want to participate to have to wait for a random call — one based, for instance, on drawing names from a jar. Thus, you may wish to indicate to students that while you will at times call on students who raise their hands, you will also *regularly* call on students who do not.

For instance, you can start a discussion by calling on students using a random method — such as names in a jar. By starting with a random method, you increase your chances that reluctant speakers will contribute their thoughts. If you start with class leaders (who may well have valuable insights to offer), some students may feel reluctant to disagree with them. A random method can be very useful if your goal is to get a variety of ideas flowing at the outset.

However, after you call on a student this way, be sure to put the slip of paper back in the jar. If you don't, the student can either become frustrated by the fact that s/he won't be called on again for a long time or feel s/he is "off the hook" for another round. By putting the name back in the jar, you prevent students from dropping out of the discussion because they know they won't be called on.

If you decide at some point in the discussion to call on volunteers, look around the room for volunteers who have not yet been heard. Making eye contact with shy students and smiling may encourage them to raise their hands to speak. To avoid calling repeatedly on the same volunteers, mix the two methods: continue to call on students randomly — even if your very vocal students have their hands in the air again — then return to calling on volunteers.

COMMUNICATION SKILLS

To feel comfortable answering and asking questions in the classroom, students require a nonjudgmental atmosphere. They must be told that there are "no stupid questions and no stupid answers," and after being told, they must see that this is so in the way their questions are handled. If students feel threatened in any way, they will not take the intellectual risks your questions require.

There are several important communication skills you can practice to put students at ease while they are speaking, encourage them to articulate their responses fully, and elicit additional responses. Some of these are discussed here.

ACTIVE LISTENING

A number of different communication skills are often referred to collectively as "active listening" skills. In contrast to silent or passive listening, the listener uses these skills to *actively* help, support, and guide the person who is speaking. You can use these skills in your classroom to encourage students to respond fully to questions and, as they do, to come to their own understanding and solutions.

> In contrast to silent or passive listening, the listener uses these skills to actively help, support, and guide the person who is speaking.

Active listening involves many different communication strategies, some of which are described below. These strategies can be used one-on-one with students or during discussion to help you better understand their responses. Most importantly, they must be applied thoughtfully — that is, your listening must guide you to your use of each strategy.

- **Mirroring** involves repeating small portions of students' statements verbatim. This technique can be useful when a student is having a difficult time expressing him/herself. Repeating a phrase of the student's response can let a struggling student know you are listening to and interested in what s/he has to say. It can also help keep the student focused and encourage elaboration. For example, in response to the question, "What steps would you have to take to solve the word problem on page 22?" a student might offer, "I'd do it backwards." Mirroring the student's response with, "You'd do it backwards…" may prompt the student to explain, "Yes, instead of multiplying like we did for the others, I'd take the total and divide."

- **Paraphrasing** involves restating or summarizing what students have said in your own words. An important caution is that too much paraphrasing during group discussion can prevent students from working to arrive at their own understandings. Thus, paraphrasing should be used when students are struggling to formulate their responses or have not provided complete or clear responses. When used this way, this strategy can prevent misunderstanding. In addition, it can communicate to students that you have heard, are trying to understand, and care about what they have said. It can also encourage clarification and elaboration. For example, in response to the question, "How are the two characters alike?" a student might offer facts without clearly connecting them: "Well, Marco's family is wealthy, but things happened to him that made him feel different. And Sheila is poor and thinks she won't make friends." Paraphrasing the student's response — for example, "Let me see if I'm understanding you… I think you're saying that even though they came from different backgrounds, they both felt like outcasts." — may help the student clarify the similarity s/he intended: "They both felt alone."

- **Clarifying** involves asking a question in order to get more information, to learn how a student is using a term, to elucidate the student's reasoning, or to connect the student's response to the question asked. This technique can be very useful when a response is unclear or when you or other students do not fully understand the response. Asking for clarification can help students dig deeper in their own thinking and ultimately arrive at new and deeper understandings. For example, in response to the student response about the two literary characters, described above, you could respond instead, "I think I see where you're going but I'm not sure. I understand how you see that Marco and Sheila were different... they had different backgrounds... but I'm not sure how you see them as being alike. Can you explain a little more?" The student may respond by clarifying, "Even though they were mostly different, they both felt alone."

- **Reflecting** involves asking a question in order to help students analyze, hypothesize, imagine, compare/contrast, extrapolate, or evaluate. This technique can be useful when a student is having a difficult time seeing "beyond" narrow circumstances. Asking students to reflect in specific ways can help them consider their ideas from new perspectives. For example, in preparing a campaign speech, a student may be unsure how to appeal to his/her peers. Asking, "What if you were a voter instead of a candidate? What would make you choose a candidate?" may help the student begin to frame his/her views.

ADDITIONAL COMMUNICATION STRATEGIES

In addition to specific active listening strategies, purposeful questioning involves many additional communication skills. The list below suggests ways you can use active listening and other communication techniques in your classroom when questioning students.

- Make sure students have completed any previous activities before you begin a questioning session. Students cannot work on other things during discussion and also listen attentively, reflect, and formulate thoughts and responses.

- Be sure you have students' attention when you pose a question. For example, if your class is large, you could move among students as you speak. Also, try to make eye contact with as many students as possible while you are speaking; it can help keep them engaged.

- Wait to call on students until *after* you have asked your question. If you call on someone first, other students may feel they don't have to think or listen.

- If the class seems restless while a student is responding, politely say, "Excuse me, ____, could you stop for a moment?" to the speaker and glance around the room. Wait a moment until the class is ready to focus on the conversation so the response can be made in a respectful atmosphere.

- If a nonvolunteer is silent or says, "I don't know." try rephrasing the question or asking a question that leads up to the original one. Avoid asking questions that put the student on the spot — such as, "Didn't you do the reading?" There are many reasons the student may be unable to formulate a response. Maintain a friendly demeanor and try to find something the student *can* respond to, but do not let the class's attention remain focused on the student for too long if s/he cannot respond.

- Make and maintain eye contact with a student while s/he is speaking to show you are listening to and interested in what s/he is saying. If you appear distracted — for example, because you are thinking about what you are going to do next — the student may cut the response short.

- In the same spirit, use nonverbal gestures to encourage the student to continue. For instance, you might nod your head, strike a "thinking" pose, or use other appropriate facial expressions.

- Never interrupt the student. Allow him/her to finish before you or someone else begin speaking.

- Wait a few seconds after you think the student has finished to be certain that s/he is indeed done. You can use this time to reflect on your understanding of the student's response. The pause may also permit the student to add to or clarify the response.

- If you did not understand the student, using probing questions — such as, "What do you mean when you say _____?" or "Could you give us an example of that?" — can help the student to clarify the response.

- If you would like the student to elaborate further, try, "Can you tell us more about that?"

- If a response is complex, or you think you understood the student but are not sure, briefly paraphrase the response. For example, you could begin, "Okay, so you think…." Then, look at the speaker and ask, "Is that right?" But again, be sure not to paraphrase students more than necessary, or students may feel they don't have to work to understand their peers, since you will be doing this work for them.

- If a response is complex, you might also want to check other students' understanding. For example, you could say, "That can be a difficult concept to grasp. Does everyone understand what _____ said?" If the response is, "No," ask students if they have questions for the speaker, ask the speaker if s/he would be willing to rephrase the response, or paraphrase a point and ask a new question based on it to bring students up to the same level of understanding.

IMPORTANT TEACHER ATTITUDES

In addition to communication skills, a few important teacher attitudes can help assure your success with questioning.

- **Keep an open mind:** Good discussion can move in many directions. While you may have a goal for student learning, it is important to keep an open mind about the path that will take students there. Try not to lead students too closely toward a foregone conclusion, and do not decide in advance how the discussion should end. In other words, be willing to follow and support students' thinking.

- **Stay positive:** Students will need cues about the quality of their responses, but negative cues can thwart future responses. Instead, offer only varying degrees of positive reinforcement. If a response is off target, still acknowledge the speaker politely. For example, you might say, "Well, that tells us _____, but right now we need to know _____." Similarly, when you see that it was difficult for a student to respond, it may be helpful to thank the student for sharing his/her thoughts. Save your praise for responses that you want other students to attend to. For instance, when a student shares an apt insight, you could say, "That's a good point, _____," and explain specifically how the point contributes to learning. From there, you can provide additional positive reinforcement by asking the class to respond to the student — for example, "Does everyone understand the point _____ just made?" or "Does anyone have a question for _____ about his/her point?"

- **Beware of empty praise:** The feedback you offer students when they respond to questions can serve as important signposts on the road to learning. For instance, praising a response and explaining the significance of the observation or the student's thinking can help all students monitor their thinking and lead them to additional insights. Thus, your feedback should be substantive; it should recognize the processes students use to generate effective responses. Too much praise, or empty praise, can encourage students to imitate an earlier response just to hear the "Good!" that response elicited. Feedback that supports student thinking, on the other hand, encourages them to try to imitate that thinking.

> The feedback you offer students when they respond to questions can serve as important signposts on the road to learning.

- **Be accepting, but also expecting:** It is important to respond positively toward — or accept — all student responses. After all, your goal is to keep student responses flowing. However, your attitude of acceptance does not mean you do not expect students to think increasingly "harder and smarter." Your role is to provide the questions and direction that help students explore beyond their initial responses, to reason more deeply, and to make connections.

- **Be aware of your own nonverbal cues:** Students respond both to what you say and how you say it. For instance, telling a student that a response is interesting while concentrating on something else contradicts your intent. The best way to stay focused on students who are responding is to practice active listening and other communication skills noted earlier.

- **Maintain your questioning stance:** If a question fails to generate responses, don't give up on your students by answering it yourself. Ask yourself, do students have what they need to answer this question? Is it too hard? Too easy? Have they had enough time to think? Consider rephrasing the question or asking a different one. Alternatively, let students work on the question in small groups and then return to discussion.

- **Express your own curiosity and enthusiasm:** When it comes to getting students excited about questions, your own thrill over a good question may be a valuable tool. Students may not always hear questions forming in their own minds. Your willingness to voice questions you suspect they may have, and your passion about the importance of those questions, can help students feel more comfortable voicing their own ideas.

- **Think of yourself as the facilitator:** While your enthusiasm for questioning can ignite students' curiosity, it is important that you keep that enthusiasm in check. Just as too much involvement from very vocal students can silence the ideas and opinions of other students, so can yours. Students may be reluctant to disagree with you, or may provide responses they think will please you. Monitor your level of involvement in student discussion, with a goal of staying in the background. Encourage students to respond to one another instead of to you.

- **Don't be judgmental:** Whether or not you agree with the student, and whether or not the response is correct, support the student's *right* to the response with your tone. As the facilitator of class discussion, your role is to help the student articulate his/her ideas. If the speaker feels right away that the response is out of favor, it could shut down not only this response but also future responses and responses of other students.

WAIT TIME

A key strategy that has been proven to increase the number of student responses to teacher questions, as well as the length and depth of those responses, is *wait time* — a silent pause of up to several seconds between voicing a question and calling on students for answers. When you ask an authentic question, most students need time to process their thoughts before they can respond. If you call on someone too soon after asking your question — or even before — some students may not formulate responses at all ("That wasn't *my* question..."). Waiting just a few seconds encourages all students to think and respond.

> When you ask an authentic question, most students need time to process their thoughts before they can respond.

While studies have shown that teachers frequently wait only about one second before asking for responses, they have also proven — at all levels of schooling — that increasing wait time to three to five seconds can produce dramatic results in the classroom.[9] In addition to prompting longer responses and bringing about increased participation, lengthening wait time helps students formulate more logical responses. After these few seconds, students become more willing to speculate and more likely to connect their claims to supporting evidence. They also become more likely to ask questions of their own.

As noted earlier, using a few seconds of wait time *after a student finishes responding to a question* can produce additional positive effects. For example, the silence may encourage students to reflect on what they said and clarify it. Alternatively, it may prompt them to ask a question or connect their thoughts with something another student said.

Depending on your level of experience, three to five seconds may seem like a long time to you. If you are unsure of the length of your pauses, count them out silently: one-one-thousand, two-one-thousand, three-one-thousand, and so on. Or, practice reflecting at this moment on the wording of your question, potential student responses, or alternative questions you can use to prompt replies. You will likely find, as other teachers have, that using "wait time" with your students is also beneficial to you.

It is important to note that using silences in the classroom can also have negative effects. While three to five seconds of wait time has been proven effective in encouraging more and deeper student responses, extending wait time too far can be demeaning. Prolonged silences can make students feel as though they have done something wrong — even if they have not. If students are unable to answer when called on, and there are few or no volunteers, your question may be unclear, too complicated, or too difficult for students. It may be time to rephrase the question or ask a new one that targets a different ability level.

If you have posed a difficult question that requires students to formulate complex responses, you may wish to vary the way you use wait time. While three seconds of wait time may support a straightforward question, and five seconds may be enough to prompt responses to some higher-level questions, complex questions may require more thought, reflection, or calculation on the part of students. Instead of a long unannounced silence, at these times tell students that you will give them a set number of seconds or minutes to think before you call on them. Alternatively, you could ask them to take a few minutes to write down some thoughts before they respond.

[9]See, for example, Rowe, M. (1974). Relation of wait-time and rewards to the development of language, logic, and fate control: Part one: Wait time. *Journal of Research in Science Teaching, 11*(2), 81-94 [Part two: Rewards. *11(4)*, 291-308.]

NEXT DIRECTIONS

After a student completes a response to a question, there are many possible next directions the discussion can take. This is where your willingness to be flexible, to listen, and to think on your feet come in. Students' responses are key to possible next directions. After a student has finished speaking, you may see a new direction right away. If you do not, you can weigh the response by asking yourself questions: Do we need additional points of view? Is there something in the response that the class can continue to pursue? Does the response suggest something about the issue that we should pause and reflect on? It may be helpful to remember that you can:

- Gather additional points of view: "Are there any other responses?" "What are some other ideas?"

- Seek a counterpoint: "Would someone with a different point of view (or different strategy) like to share it with the class?"

- Up the ante: Ask a higher level question using the response as a transition.

- Suggest a new direction: "In light of what _____ said, I find myself wondering what/how/when/why/where/whether…. Does anyone have any ideas?"

- Encourage linking: "Does what _____ said remind you of anything we have been talking about recently?"

- Suggest a metacognitive connection: "Wow, that's an interesting insight. Has anyone else experienced that?" Then, "What does that suggest about how we learn?"

- Give students an opportunity to ask questions: "Does anyone have a question for _____ about his/her response?" or "Who would like to ask a question about the topic we've been discussing?"

POTENTIAL OBSTACLES TO SUCCESSFUL QUESTIONING AND DISCUSSION

A full discussion of potential obstacles to questioning is beyond the scope of this minicourse. While many teachers may encounter similar kinds of obstacles, most situations differ due to particular characteristics of individuals and school districts. Nonetheless, it is important that you consider the potential obstacles in your unique setting and plan for them when implementing new teaching strategies.

Some potential obstacles may be easily solved. For instance, if you have an especially verbal class, your obstacle may not be starting discussion but stopping or controlling it. Potential solutions may include using a two-minute egg timer to help moderate discussion, or ending discussion with a free-writing exercise that allows students to express lingering thoughts.

However, other obstacles may be outside your control. For example, your class may be very large or of vastly mixed ability levels. You may struggle with students who come to class unprepared or you may be burdened by unusually demanding curriculum requirements. Your students' cultural values may discourage questioning, or students may be resistant to questioning for other reasons.

All of these potential obstacles place legitimate concerns in your path as you strive to improve your use of questioning and discussion strategies with students. However, the importance of questioning to the development of student thinking makes it imperative that you address and overcome potential obstacles. Students need questions to stimulate their thinking and to help them learn to solve problems. They need to know that they *can* question and that their questions can drive their own learning. The questions you ask students, the questions you ask them to frame, and the discussion opportunities that you provide are critical rehearsals for work they will do later in their professional and personal lives.

> The questions you ask students, the questions you ask them to frame, and the discussion opportunities that you provide are critical rehearsals for work they will do later in their professional and personal lives.

In Related Activities for the Teacher, which follow, you will have an opportunity to reflect on potential obstacles in your environment as well as possible solutions to them. It may help to remember that you should expect to make incremental progress in this and other areas, and that other teachers can be a key resource in overcoming potential obstacles.

Directions: The following activities are intended to help you reflect on your current interpersonal skills and classroom climate and to help you identify goals and potential obstacles in these areas. These activities should be completed sequentially and in a manner conducive to your own individual learning style.

		COMPLETED
1	Using **My Minicourse Journal**, which follows, reflect on your current methods of interacting with students and your present classroom environment. Questions are provided to guide your reflection.	
2	What would you *like* to be able to say about your communication skills or classroom environment at some point in the future? In the **My Goals for Climates and Attitudes** chart, which follows, list in the column labeled *Goals* three to five measurable claims you would like to be able to make, and suggest in the column labeled *Activities* two to four steps you can take toward your goals.	
3	In the **Potential Obstacles** chart, which follows, brainstorm any possible obstacles you see to implementing deeper questioning strategies with your students, in the column labeled *Obstacles*. If you wish, in the *Notes* column you may add ideas you have now about solutions — or even just reminders to yourself, such as, "Ask so-and-so what s/he does about this." These obstacles will be considered again in Part IV when you plan a lesson supported by questions.	

4   If you wish, discuss your thoughts with other teachers. If you are a member of a study group, you may want to suggest completing activity 3 together. After brainstorming potential obstacles individually, discuss potential solutions as a group. Take notes during the discussion in the **What I Learned From Other Teachers** chart to help you recall what was said. The following questions about potential obstacles may help start a professional conversation:

- What do you do when a student response is funny?

- What if a student is so comfortable speaking that s/he doesn't stop?

- What if a student is having a hard time articulating a response?

- What if a student gives the answer to the question before the other students even get warmed up?

my minicourse
Journal

1. Is my physical environment conducive to discussion?

2. Are my students comfortable speaking their minds?

3. What is the pace of my questioning? Do I give students enough wait time?

4. What kinds of things do I do or say to encourage responses from more students?

5. What can I do to elicit deeper responses and fuller discussion from students?

6. What do my students need from their environment to begin a new level of questioning?

My Goals for Climates and Attitudes

GOALS	ACTIVITIES
Example: *I would like to increase the number of students who contribute to class discussions.*	Example: *1. Call on more nonvolunteers.* *2. Call on nonvolunteers first.* *3. Use more student questions.* *4. Allow students to respond to questions in groups or pairs more frequently.*

OBSTACLES	NOTES
Example: *Several of my students continually come to class unprepared. How can I motivate them to take an interest in learning and contribute to class discussion?*	Example: • *Consult with students' parents and their other teachers.* • *Provide some start-to-finish activities in school. Place students in groups to prepare for questioning together, but make everyone responsible for contributing to discussion.*

What I Learned From Other Teachers

TEACHER	INPUT

BUILDING STUDENT COMFORT WITH QUESTIONING

Before pursuing a new questioning strategy with students, it is a good idea to discuss your approach with them so that they know what to expect. For example, you could start by explaining your belief that learning is most effective when students are permitted to arrive at it on their own. You could then describe how questions and resulting discussions help students think and learn. You may also wish to distinguish between discussion and debate: the goal is exploration — learning — not proving who is right and who is wrong.

If your students are new to questioning, it may also be helpful to lead them in nonthreatening activities that can help accustom them to questioning (see Related Activities for Students at the end of this chapter). When first faced with the prospect of sharing their thoughts in a class setting, some students may be alarmed by thoughts of potential embarrassment. Others may fear "failing" at your new approach. Leading students in practice activities that do not threaten their grades and do not require risky disclosure can increase their confidence, quell their fears, and leave them excited about questioning.

The remaining sections of Part III are all concerned with building student comfort with questioning.

ESTABLISHING GROUND RULES WITH STUDENTS

Have you ever heard congressional or parliamentary leaders speak to one another in a formal session? For example, before beginning to address the governing body, you may have heard a representative first say, "Thank you, Mr./Madame Speaker" to the previous spokesperson. Even when strongly disagreeing with another speaker, the representative may refer to him/her as "my esteemed colleague." This practiced tone of civility may sometimes seem stilted, but it imparts a sense of order and depersonalizes heated discussions among people with very different points of view.

> Ground rules introduce students to appropriate behaviors and attitudes that make it possible for each of them to share their points of view, and are essential to provocative discussion.

Similarly, ground rules for class discussion provide a safe environment in which students may express themselves. Ground rules introduce students to appropriate behaviors and attitudes that make it possible for each of them to share their points of view, and are essential to provocative discussion. Ground rules for classroom questioning and discussion serve students two ways:

1. **Manners of discussion** ensure that students' are treated respectfully when sharing their ideas and opinions. For example:

- Listen respectfully and silently when someone is speaking.

- Make a good faith effort to understand your peers' points of view.

- If you do not understand another student's statement, respond by asking a question.

- Show respect for cultural differences, students' opinions, and other student values.

- When responding to others, use polite speech — such as, "I think I see what you are saying, but ..." — before countering.

- Wait for a speaker to finish before raising your hand.

2. **Habits of mind** help students understand mindsets that lead to productive, and provocative, discussion. For example:

- Always be honest — say what you believe.

- Take risks — push yourself to share your thoughts.

- Try to be clear — be willing to explain your thinking and answer questions.

- Keep an open mind — be willing to question things you take for granted.

- Challenge your own thinking by looking for evidence.

- Stay on topic.

- Ask yourself whether something has to be true for everyone.

- Side with other students because you truly agree with them, not because they are friends.

- When you have the floor, take time to express yourself, but remember that others also wish to speak.

- If we cannot come to a consensus, agree to disagree.

In order for all students to feel comfortable contributing to discussion, it is a good idea to enlist their help in establishing the code of behavior that will support them during discussion. This way, every student has an opportunity to suggest the support s/he needs. One way to do this is suggested in Related Activities for Students at the end of Part III. If students are new to questioning, this activity can help them better understand the group commitment they will make to challenge their collective thinking.[10]

---

[10]Depending on your curricular goals, you could also explore other sets of ground rules at this time — such as Robert's Rules of Order, originally devised in 1915 to regulate parliamentary discussions.

The time you choose to establish ground rules with students can also be a good time to explain to them the methods you will use to call on them to speak, discussed earlier. You may also want to tell them what they can expect from you in the course of discussion. For example:

■ I will apply the ground rules fairly.

■ I will be open to all points of view.

■ I will take your opinions and ideas seriously.

■ I will do everything in my power to give everyone a chance to be heard.

After establishing ground rules with your students, return to them periodically as a means of asking the class to assess its discussion behavior. For example, after telling the class, "Now that you have some experience with discussion, let's review our ground rules," you could ask them:

■ Which ground rules are most important?

■ Which ground rules are hardest to follow?

■ Are our ground rules appropriate for our needs?

■ Are there behaviors we can add to encourage more sharing?

■ Are there habits of mind we can add that might encourage deeper discussion?

■ Are there any ground rules that are preventing better discussion?

Be sure to remind students not to mention the behavior of specific students during this discussion, but to speak generally. If the class is struggling to control negative behaviors, you may also want to ask each student to write a discussion goal for him or herself that he/she will not be required to share with the class.

HELPING STUDENTS ASK QUESTIONS

One area in which students will need your structured support is generating their own questions. While naturally curious, students who are not accustomed to questioning will not know what is expected of them in this area without some assistance. If you started using questioning with your students before this time, they may already be familiar with the language of questions and may be eager to begin formulating their own. Nonetheless, because questions can take so many forms, they will still need guidance in drafting questions that are both meaningful to them and suited to your instructional purposes.

> *Using content that students have mastered provides them with an opportunity to focus exclusively on posing their own questions.*

Some tools you can use to introduce your students to the art of framing questions are described in Related Activities for Students at the end of Part III. These are intended to provide students with structured opportunities to frame questions before they are asked to generate them in the context of a lesson and, later, when they are asked to frame specific types of questions for a particular lesson.

For example, the Model and Practice activity uses a story — such as a fairy tale or other children's book — that is well known to students to model the process of formulating questions and to provide them with practice in writing questions. Using content that students have mastered provides them with an opportunity to focus exclusively on posing their own questions. Children's stories are effective for this activity. While they are familiar to students, they also inspire a well of questions when viewed in new ways.

When students first begin composing questions, "something you are curious about" may be your only requirement. But later, you may wish to broaden the range of question types students ask, or to have them write particular types of questions for specific purposes. The various Taxonomy activities and the Word Banks activity support students' efforts to frame specific kinds of questions in the context of a lesson. These activities — which are intended for students who have some experience asking questions — can help students formulate the kinds of questions you intend and can strengthen students' understanding of the questions you ask.

USING STUDENT-GENERATED QUESTIONS

One important way you can support your students and their learning is by using their questions to scaffold your teaching. Your lessons present numerous opportunities for students to generate questions as well as for you to incorporate student questions into your lessons. Related Activities for Students at the end of Part III suggest ways you can incorporate student questions into lessons.

The first opportunity you have to elicit student questions is when you first introduce a lesson. Whether or not students have any prior knowledge of the topic, their questions will likely broach aspects of the lesson that you feel are important. For instance, if you plan to introduce students to percentages for the first time, students may ask, "What is a percentage?" "What do we use percentages for?" "How do you figure out percentages?" These questions may not lead you to approach your lesson differently, but by using students' questions to introduce the aspects of the lesson to which they relate, you can increase their attentiveness to important points you wish to make. At the beginning of an explanation of when we use percentages, for instance, you might remind students, "Okay, several of you asked, 'What do we use percentages for?' Let's talk about that now. Has anyone heard or seen percentages being used?" Their responses will likely take you to a discussion of sale prices, tips, opinion polls, and more.

Depending on the new content students are about to learn, you may also find that early student questions can help you determine which of many possible topical issues will guide your class discussions. For example, if you are about to introduce a novel to students — say, *The Last of the Mohicans* — a student could ask, "How could Cooper know someone was the 'last' Mohican?" or "What would it feel like to be the only one left of your tribe?" Such questions provide important clues as to what matters to students and can be used to focus discussion — in this case, an investigation into the treatment of specific groups in both literature and in our culture.

A second opportunity for students to ask questions arises after some initial learning on a topic has taken place. When students use their prior learning to inform their questions, that learning is reflected in their questions and can be used to drive their understanding to deeper levels. For instance, after initial lessons in percentages, students may ask, "Is there a quicker way to figure percentages?" or "If 50% is the same as half, why don't we just use the fraction?" You can use such questions to introduce students to "mental math" shortcuts and to tie their understanding of percentages to the concept of fractions.

A third opportunity presents itself after significant learning takes place. At this juncture — especially if discussion played a role in the learning — students may have begun to consider new points of view as well as new content, skills, and ideas. The questions they ask at this point in their learning may be useful for framing projects or inspiring creativity. For example — in response to the question, "Now that you know about percentages, what questions do you have about how they are used?" — a student might ask, "How do newspaper reporters know that a certain percentage of people plan to vote for a particular candidate? Do they ask everyone?" Such a question can undergird a class project on poll taking.

Similarly, speculative questions — "What if you were the last representative of your culture?" — can provide inspiring ideas for creative projects, such as poems, essays, stories, posters, photo-essays, collages, and so on. It is not necessary for students to always respond verbally to questions. Visual/graphical responses can be equally compelling, and can provide alternative outlets for students who prefer visual means of expression to verbal means. In addition, creative projects driven by students' speculative and other post-learning questions provide opportunities for them to express the emotions, opinions, and ideals that developed around their new learning.

Reminders and Tips About Student-Generated Questions

- Using student questions to enrich discussion does not mean that you give up control of the direction of student learning. On the contrary, when you ask students to frame questions, you maintain control over how and when they are used.

- You can use student questions in combination with your own questions — for instance, in place of similar questions you intended to ask anyway; to help you choose which issues to pursue in discussion; or even to take discussion in relevant, unplanned directions.

- Ask older students to write their questions on note cards so that you can easily review them and pull out a few to use in class. Be sure to remind students to include their names so they can be credited for their questions when you use them. (Since this is another way of participating in discussion, using student questions can be an effective way to involve reluctant speakers.)

- Record younger students' questions on chart paper or the chalk board as they generate them. Ask them to help you combine similar questions. Leave questions visible during lessons so you can refer to them when you address them.

- Strive to use questions from as many different students as possible. Students take significant pride in hearing their questions asked in class. Record the names of students whose questions you use to help you keep track of students who have not had turns.

- As you use student questions, encourage metacognitive reflection. Point out how their questions build on previous learning or questions, and ask what they must do to answer their own questions.

- When asking students to compose questions, always ask them to write two or three to encourage them to think beyond the first question that comes into their heads.

RESPONDING TO STUDENT QUESTIONS

When you use a student question to fuel discussion in a planned manner, it is easy to see that the response will be collaborative — the class will use it as a starting place for group inquiry. However, at other times, students will turn specifically to you with their questions. It is important to remember that how you respond to student questions can impact students' comfort with questioning either positively or negatively.

When a student turns to you, one-on-one, with questions, you can use the strategies noted earlier to listen effectively, probe, and direct the student with appropriate follow-up questions, checking later to see if the response satisfied the student. Similarly, when students turn to you with questions during discussion, you may readily see how you can respond. For example, a student question may arise from content and can be used on the spot to turn discussion in still another productive direction; you can redirect the question to the class, or help the student answer his/her own question by using listening and prompting strategies described earlier. Fact-checking or clarification questions can also be turned over to students — though time constraints may sometimes make it more prudent for you to provide the answer so that students may continue in a more investigative direction. If the question raises a tangential point, you may wish to defer the question to a later time, but be sure to note both the student and the question so that the "later time" actually arrives.

At other times, however, you may sense that the motivation for students' questions is not content-based. For example, students may be seeking clarity with their questions in situations that are intrinsically unclear. They may want to know "who's right and who's wrong." Or they may want an arbitrator who can "make the other students understand." Discussion, especially when it broaches issues of value or belief, can be very uncomfortable for students, and their initial reactions may be to try to "make the discomfort go away."

These kinds of questions can be very challenging, especially if you feel strongly about an opinion under discussion. However, it is critical that you stay in the background, because "taking sides" will cause you to alienate at least part of the class and would be a breach of your promise to be fair and nonjudgmental. It is important to remember that these types of questions provide an opportunity for you to help students learn that some discussions close without resolution.

> As you use student questions, encourage metacognitive reflection. Point out how their questions build on previous learning or questions, and ask what they must do to answer their own questions.

When this occurs during discussions of "big issues," it can be helpful to remind students that the same conflicts they are experiencing have fueled arguments among philosophers, religious leaders, or nations from the beginning of time. You may wish to appeal to their desire for peacefulness by relating what can happen when dialogues break down and asking for their ideas on more satisfying solutions. Ask them what strategies they think people with deeply entrenched differences use to live side-by-side with one another. And remind them that they are all entitled to their opinions, to personal safety, and to other liberties, regardless of their beliefs.

Avoiding Responses That May Alienate Students

In addition to taking sides, a few other teacher responses have the potential to alienate students. For example, answering an opinion question definitively, providing an answer when you are actually unsure, and becoming frustrated over their queries or responses can cause students to lose their willingness to trust you with their authentic questions.

Holding Back Your Opinion

Students who come to you with opinion questions — and who may at these times even ask your opinion directly or indirectly — are most likely struggling with forming their own opinions. Even when talking one-on-one with students about these issues, it may generally be better to maintain your facilitator, or background, attitude, rather than give your opinion. Your listening skills, and your well-chosen questions aimed at helping the student reflect productively on the topic, can free the student to settle upon his/her own opinion as well as provide the tools to do so.

> Your listening skills, and your well-chosen questions aimed at helping the student reflect productively on the topic, can free the student to settle upon his/her own opinion as well as provide the tools to do so.

When You Don't Know the Answer...

Not knowing the answer to a student question may sometimes feel unsettling. One possible initial reaction is to fear that the student will lose respect for you as an information authority if you cannot answer a question. However, students realize that no one knows everything, and the nonintuitive outcome in this situation is that the student will most likely respect you for your honesty. A fictional response, on the other hand, is almost guaranteed to diminish your rapport with the student.

When you don't know the answer to a question, the best response is to admit it. However, don't let the dialogue end there. A good response may be, "That's a good question... I'm not sure of the answer, but I'll bet I know how we can find out." If appropriate, you can direct the question to the class, suggest ways the student can find the information (for example, by consulting other authorities or resources), or tell the student that you would like to inquire about the question yourself. No matter which response you choose, follow up to be sure the student got the information s/he needed. For example, if you refer the student to another authority, the student's failure to ask the question of that authority may seem like a lack of motivation, but may actually be a lack of experience speaking with adults s/he doesn't know. There may be more you can do to help the student find an answer.

COPING WITH FRUSTRATION

Frustration can sometimes be a natural response to continuous questioning. However, if you feel frustrated, it is important that you keep it in check. Expressing your frustration with student questions will counteract the work you are doing to advance student questioning.

Instead of expressing your frustration, use it as an indicator. When you sense your frustration, look around and ask yourself why you are feeling that way. Sometimes the source of the frustration may be that the question comes at a bad time. If you recognize that this is so, give the student a time when it would be more appropriate to have the discussion. Similarly, you may feel frustrated that the same students volunteer to respond over and over again. In this case, it is important not to "blame" students "for being good." If you find you are frustrated with generous responders, thank these students politely for their untiring willingness to participate, but note that you would also like to hear from other students.

On the other hand, if you feel frustrated because you feel you have already answered the question, or because the student seems not to understand something when other indicators show s/he does, chances are good that the student does not know how to articulate the question that is actually stirring him/her. Use your probing strategies to unearth the source of misunderstanding. Remember, though, this may not occur easily. It may take time for the student to respond to your mirroring strategies and your questions, and to arrive at the question at the heart of his/her confusion. Sometimes, the best you may be able to do is to keep trying in good faith.

Similarly, some student questions or responses can seem at first to be wildly off-topic. Yet, sometimes students make several steps in their thinking in response to questions and verbalize only the conclusion they reached — making the question or response seem tangential or abbreviated. At these times, resist dismissing the response and instead ask the student to clarify and elaborate his/her thinking.

BUILDING STUDENTS' AWARENESS OF THEIR THINKING PROCESSES

In the course of questioning, it is important to encourage students to examine their own thinking processes by asking them to reflect on or explain how they arrived at their ideas or answers. Heightened awareness of their individual thinking and learning processes can help students become more successful in school — as well as beyond school.

> *In the course of questioning, it is important to encourage students to examine their own thinking processes by asking them to reflect on or explain how they arrived at their ideas or answers.*

For example, when students who repeatedly make careless errors on math tests are asked, "What goes on in your mind during a test?" they may realize that they respond to time pressure by rushing. A logical next question — "What can you do to slow yourself down?" — can help students find ways to gain control over this initial reaction.

Similarly, by recognizing through metacognitive reflection that a path s/he took in planning an experiment was "deductive," a student may be better equipped to consider that path strategically the next time s/he plans an investigation.

The Cycle of Metacognitive Reflection

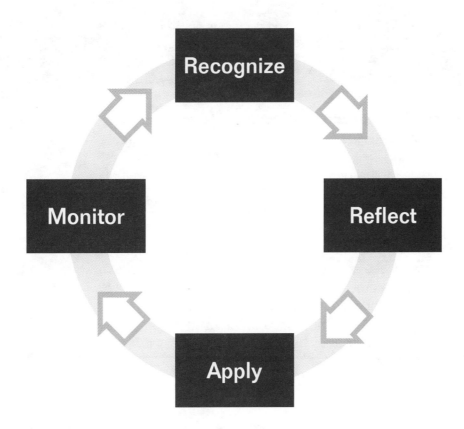

Students gain understanding of their thinking and learning processes in four stages, which they repeat as they learn:

- First, they **recognize** what they do, think, or feel when they are learning; how they evaluate a situation or imagine an outcome; or how they plan or proceed when solving a problem.

- Second, they **reflect** on how what they do changes, affects, impacts, helps, or hurts their success, as well as how they might respond differently next time or use their self-awareness in a new situation.

- Third, they **apply** their new awareness in subsequent learning situations.

- Fourth, they continue to **monitor** their thinking and learning in a continuous cycle.

Your questions can guide and support students at every stage of this important learning process.

KWL Chart
Page 95
Chapter 96

Directions: The following activities are designed to help students become accustomed to questioning in a non-threatening, supportive manner.

COMPLETED

1 **Establishing Ground Rules With Students.** By pointing out to students that not everyone is comfortable at first with offering their thoughts in a class setting, you can set the stage for this group activity. Begin by explaining that the ground rules the class establishes will support each of them when they speak. Ask them, "What behaviors are important if we are all to feel comfortable expressing our thoughts and opinions?" As students brainstorm, chart their responses and encourage them to collapse similar responses in order to keep the list manageable.[11] It may be helpful to provide an "Examples" column in the chart so that duplicate contributions can be used in some way. Also, the examples may help illuminate the rules for some students.

Sample chart:

Manners of Discussion	
RULE	EXAMPLE
Example: *Listen silently when someone is speaking.*	Example: *Don't interrupt.* *Don't boo or cheer.*

[11]The number of ground rules should vary with students' grade level. Also, ground rules should place *reasonable* limitations on behavior; dissuade students from making the rules overly restrictive.

Use questions, or provide scenarios, to elicit additional rules from students until you feel that all important manners of discussion have been considered. For example, to elicit a rule on respecting differences, you could ask students, "What if someone comes from a cultural background that is very different than yours? What behaviors will help this person feel comfortable expressing his or her thoughts and opinions?"

Habits of Mind. Next, introduce the habits of mind that are important to productive discussion. Students who are unaccustomed to questioning may need more assistance with these. Provide an example to get them started. Again, use questions and scenarios to help students generate the habits of mind that are important to good discussion. For instance, "What if someone has an opinion that conflicts very strongly with yours? How can we prevent our disagreements from hurting friendships?"

Sample chart:

Habits of Mind	
RULE	EXAMPLE
Example: *Keep an open mind.*	Example: *Remember there are many points of view.* *No one is "right" when it comes to values and opinions.*

2 **Activities That Build Student Comfort With Questioning.** Use the following activities to help accustom your students to questioning before implementing your new strategy. Depending on your students' needs, you may use one or all of these activities; they are suggested in order of students' increasing comfort with questioning.

■ **Illustrate the benefits of discussion with a teambuilding activity.** If students are new to the idea of sharing responses as a group, it may help to break the ice with a teambuilding activity, such as the yarn toss. Start by asking students a nonthreatening question — such as "How do you think we can increase school spirit?" (If you know students are conflicted on this issue, choose another question.) Explain that you will give the first response, then you will toss a ball of yarn to a student (whom you choose randomly) while still holding on to the string. The student holding the yarn will then respond to the question and, when finished, will toss the ball to another student, also continuing to hold the string — and so on around the room until everyone responds. As students share responses, a yarn web forms, which you can use to physically illustrate the concept of discussion. Explain that the web shows how connected students are in their thinking; how their responses to questions can help each other; how important the thoughts and opinions of each individual are to the group; and how important it is to the discussion that everyone holds up his/her "piece of string."

■ **Lead a practice discussion.** Choose a topic that students have mastered and question them on that topic. Use the **Practice Discussion** chart, which follows, to plan questions at various levels to illustrate a range of questioning strategies. Continuing to use the topic as an example, describe for students the homework and projects related to questioning that they might be asked to complete.

■ **Let student interest be your guide.** Use the **Student Interests** chart, which follows, to plan questions that are directed at learning what interests, confuses, pleases, troubles, or inspires students about a lesson. Use what you learn to plan and lead a discussion around something of interest to them.

■ **Let students work in groups.** When students are new to discussion, or your questions require complex thinking, allow students to formulate responses to questions in small work groups. Ask all individuals in the groups to take turns sharing responses with the class so that everyone has a chance to practice speaking in front of the class. Plan this activity in the **Group Work** chart, which follows.

■ **Let students "free write" or "problem solve" first.** To provide a transition from group work to individual work, allow students to free write or problem solve in response to a question before asking for responses. Use the **Free Writing/Problem Solving** chart, which follows, to plan this activity.

TOPIC	PRACTICE DISCUSSION
POSSIBLE QUESTIONS:	
EXAMPLE HOMEWORK:	
EXAMPLE PROJECT:	

TOPIC	STUDENT INTERESTS
QUESTIONS TO ELICIT STUDENT INTERESTS:	Example: *"What about _____ most interests you?" (or "... are you most curious about?")*
WHAT I LEARNED ABOUT STUDENT INTERESTS:	
POSSIBLE DISCUSSION QUESTIONS:	

TOPIC	GROUP WORK
POSSIBLE QUESTION:	
PLANNING NOTES:	

TOPIC	FREE WRITING / PROBLEM SOLVING
POSSIBLE QUESTION:	
PLANNING NOTES:	

3 **Activities That Help Students Ask Questions.** Use the following activities to help accustom your students to asking questions that you can use to drive instruction. Depending on your students' needs, you may use one or all of these activities. Use the Model and Practice activity *before* students are asked to generate questions in the context of an actual lesson. Use the various Taxonomy activities and the Word Banks activity later — when students have some experience asking questions. These are intended to prepare students to frame specific types of questions in the context of a lesson and to think more deeply about questioning.

■ **Model and Practice.** Explain to students that you would like to begin using their questions about their learning to enrich class discussions. Next, introduce a children's story or fairy tale with which they are already very familiar[12] (for example, *The Three Little Pigs* or *The Cat in the Hat*[13]) and explain that you will use it to conduct a practice exercise. Place at least one copy of the book in a central location for students to reference. Give students a few minutes to write down questions about the tale that they are truly curious about. Explain that "answerability" is not an issue. Offer a question of your own as an example — for instance, "How did the little pigs feel when their mother told them it was time to go out and make their way in the world?" or "Is the cat dangerous or fun?" Students will likely ask a range of questions, such as, "How did the pigs learn to build houses?" or "Where does the cat come from?" Ask them to share their questions as a class, and use one or two to conduct a brief discussion. Conclude the exercise by informing students that at different points in their learning, you will ask them to prepare questions to be used in class discussions.

[12]Due to cultural differences, it's a good idea not to assume everyone is familiar with even very popular tales. Before conducting this activity, ask if everyone is familiar with the story — or ask for student input in choosing it.
[13]Geisel, Theodore (aka Dr. Seuss). (1957). *The cat in the hat.* New York: Random House.

■ **Provide a Simplified Taxonomy.** Take some time to think about the kinds of questions you would like your students to be asking. Then, provide them with a simplified taxonomy that describes the kinds of questions you want them to formulate. After introducing this framework, ask students to generate example questions and chart their responses to be sure they understand the taxonomy. Later, use the taxonomy to ask students to think of specific questions in the context of a lesson. For example, young students can distinguish "who," "what," "when," "where," "why," and "how" questions. After students are familiar with this taxonomy, you could ask them, as part of a social studies lesson, to pose as historical figures and to interview each other using their "who," "what," "when," and "where" questions for information gathering. In the context of a science or math lesson, you could ask them to formulate "how" and "why" questions to generate ideas for analysis and experimentation.

Sample chart:

	SIMPLIFIED TAXONOMY
QUESTION TYPE	STUDENTS' EXAMPLES
"WHO?"	Example: *"Who are you?"*
"WHAT?"	
"WHEN?"	
"WHERE?"	
"WHY?"	
"HOW?"	

■ **Build a Class Taxonomy.** Older students can understand and use more complex categorizations. To help them understand the idea of question types, build a taxonomy as a class. Using questions generated in the Model and Practice exercise, ask students to think about "how questions are similar" and "how questions are different." Ask them to suggest possible groupings. For example, students might come up with "pig questions," "wolf questions," "questions about feelings," "questions about what happens after the story ends," and "questions about what happened before the story started." Chart the categories students suggest for each question to illustrate that one question can be grouped into multiple categories. After students suggest many categories, ask them to consider ways their categories could be grouped.

Sample chart:

Class Taxonomy	
QUESTION	POSSIBLE CATEGORIES
Example: *"How did the pigs learn to build houses?"*	Examples: • *pig questions* • *questions about what happened before the story started*

■ **Provide Your Taxonomy.** To strengthen students'
understanding of the questions you ask, introduce
them to a particular taxonomy you use. Explain how
questions can direct specific thinking tasks. Start by
giving an example question. For instance, ask,
"What do you think is going to happen in the next
chapter of our book?" Then, explain that the
question asks students to *predict* an event. Continue
to give examples of questions, asking students to
indicate the thinking task that is required to answer
each one. Chart the different thinking tasks they
come up with on the board. Collapse similar
categories so that the taxonomy is not overly
complicated. If important question types are missing
from the taxonomy, provide examples and help
students understand the various levels of complexity
that questions can suggest. When you are through,
distribute copies of your taxonomy for students' later
reference, and let students know that from time to
time you will ask them to compose questions of a
specific type using the taxonomy.

Sample chart:

Teacher's Taxonomy	
QUESTION	THINKING TASK
Example: *"What do you think is going to happen next?"*	Examples: *predict, think ahead*

■ **Provide Directed Practice.** At times, it may be useful to elicit particular *types* of student questions for a targeted purpose. Depending on students' ages, there are several ways you can limit their questions to specific types. For example, to assess how well young students understand a math concept, you might ask strictly for "How do I … ?" or "What happens when I … ?" questions. In answering their questions, you can then provide a focused review that will benefit the entire class. Similarly, to generate ideas for discussion, research papers, or group projects in history or language arts, you may want older students to compose only "comparison" or "contrast" questions. Plan your directed practice opportunity in the **Directed Practice** chart below.

DIRECTED PRACTICE	
PURPOSE OF QUESTIONS:	
TYPE OF QUESTIONS:	
PLANNING NOTES:	

■ **Provide Word Banks.** Another approach you can use to expand the range of questions that students ask is to provide them with word banks you want them to use to frame their questions. For example, if you want students to ask more challenging questions, you could give them examples of question stems, verbs, and objects that direct specific thinking tasks. Limit your word banks, based on the grade level and abilities of your students and also based on the types of questions you would like them to ask. For example, based on the example above, you could provide the following word bank to students. Plan your word bank in the **My Student Word Bank** chart below.

QUESTION STEM	VERB	OBJECT
How do I ... ?"	add, calculate, divide, subtract, multiply, remember the steps	fractions, decimals, one-digit/two-digit/three-digit numbers, the process
"What happens when I ... ?"	change, forget, reverse, start at the end/in the middle	

MY STUDENT WORD BANK		
PURPOSE:		
QUESTION STEMS	VERBS	OBJECTS

4 **Using Student-Generated Questions to Support Learning.** Use the following activities to incorporate student questions into your lessons before initial learning, after initial learning, and after significant learning.

■ **Before Initial Learning.** Tap into students' curiosity by introducing the topic they will be learning about and asking them questions before any new learning takes place. For example, you could ask, "What do you want to know about _____?" or "What questions could we ask about _____?" Use chart paper to record young students' responses (one per page), and ask older students to write their questions on note cards. Let students know that you plan to use their questions throughout the lesson, and that the class will have an opportunity later to reflect on the answers. Review students' questions, clip similar questions together as one, place questions in the logical order in which they will most likely be answered, and number them. Use the **Before Initial Learning** chart, which follows, to plan how you will incorporate students' questions into your planned lesson. (For example, you can use them to introduce lesson subtopics, or to provide a focus for group work, discussion, research, papers, projects, or homework.) Try to use as many questions as possible, and keep the **Before Initial Learning** chart as a record of students whose questions were used.

■ **After Initial Learning.** When you return to a topic in pursuit of deeper understanding, ask students, "Now that you understand something about _____, what questions could we ask?" Alternatively, you might ask students to write a few questions on note cards for homework. You may wish to specify a particular kind of question — such as, comparison/contrast questions — and to relate the questions to specific class work or other homework. For instance, "After reading chapter two, write two questions that invite us to compare or contrast (character) and (character)." Or, "After you solve the problems, write two questions that encourage us to compare this new skill with others we have learned." Review students' questions and select those you will use to drive deeper learning. As above, clip similar questions as one, place them in logical order, and number them. Use the **After Initial Learning** chart, which follows, to plan how you will use students' questions to challenge their thinking with discussion, group work, research, papers, and projects. Try to use as many questions as possible, and keep the **After Initial Learning** chart as a record of students whose questions were used.

■ **After Significant Learning.** At the conclusion of significant learning, ask students, "Now that you know about _____, what questions do you have?" The questions they ask at this point in their learning can raise big — sometimes unanswerable — issues, and may inspire real-world simulations as well as creative expressions. As above, collect and review students' questions. Use the **After Significant Learning** chart, which follows, to plan how you will use these questions to inspire them to synthesize their thoughts and opinions, conduct simulations, or as inspiration for poems, essays, stories, posters, photo-essays, collages, and projects. Try to use as many questions as possible (for example, you could use several at once by providing students with a list of possible essay/project topics, all inspired by student questions, then asking students to each choose one). Keep the **After Significant Learning** chart as a record of students whose questions were used.

QUESTION NUMBER/ STUDENT NAME	ACTIVITY
Example: *Question 1.* *Clarissa P., David M., Esperanza F.* *("What is a percentage?")*	Example: *Introduce lesson.*
QUESTION 1.	
QUESTION 2.	
QUESTION 3.	
QUESTION 4.	
QUESTION 5.	
QUESTION 6.	
QUESTION 7.	
QUESTION 8.	
QUESTION 9.	
QUESTION 10.	

QUESTION NUMBER/ STUDENT NAME	ACTIVITY
Example: Question 1. *Christina S.* *("If 50% is the same as half, why don't we just use the fraction?")*	Example: *Introduce mental-math shortcuts for solving percentages.* *Have students work in groups to compare solving problems using percents and fraction shortcuts.* *Hold discussion: When is it faster to work with percents and when is it faster to use fraction shortcuts?*
QUESTION 1.	
QUESTION 2.	
QUESTION 3.	
QUESTION 4.	
QUESTION 5.	
QUESTION 6.	
QUESTION 7.	
QUESTION 8.	
QUESTION 9.	
QUESTION 10.	

QUESTION NUMBER/ STUDENT NAME	ACTIVITY
Example: *Question 1. Jin W., Mark B.* *("How do newspaper reporters know that a certain percentage of people plan to vote for a particular candidate? Do they ask everyone?")*	Example: *Introduce concepts of statistics, opinion polls, sampling, generalizing. Have students work in groups to conduct a poll on an issue of interest to them. As part of design, ask each group to randomly select five students to be asked their opinion about the issue (limit one question per group). Then have each group write a brief "news" article generalizing what the five said to the whole class. Hold discussion of differences between students' poll and real world poll-taking. Also discuss strengths and weaknesses of polls.*
QUESTION 1.	
QUESTION 2.	
QUESTION 3.	
QUESTION 4.	
QUESTION 5.	
QUESTION 6.	
QUESTION 7.	
QUESTION 8.	
QUESTION 9.	
QUESTION 10.	

5 **Activities That Encourage Metacognitive Reflection.**
Use the following activities to encourage students to
reflect on how they think and learn. In addition to the
activities suggested below, the Taxonomy questions
provided in activity 3 (*Activities That Help Students
Ask Questions*) can help students think more deeply
about ways that questioning supports their thinking
and learning.

- **Reflect on Student Learning Using a K-W-L Chart.**[14]
One way to help students see how their questions
fuel their learning (and simultaneously review new
learning) is to use a **K-W-L** chart. Before new
learning takes place, conduct a discussion with
students by asking them, "What do you already
know about ____ (the new content)?" Record their
responses in the "What I already KNOW" column of
the K-W-L chart. Next, ask them, "What do you
WANT to know about ____ (the new content)?"
Record their questions in the "What I WANT to
learn" column of the K-W-L chart. Incorporate these
questions into the lesson, as described earlier under
activity 4 (*Using Student-Generated Questions to
Support Learning*). Then, after the new learning
takes place, review the questions students asked
in the "What I WANT to learn" column of the K-W-L
chart. For each one, ask students, "What have you
LEARNED about ____ (student question)?" Record
their answers in the "What I LEARNED" column of
the K-W-L chart.

continued on page 96

---

[14]Ogle, D.M. (1986). K-W-L: A teaching model that develops active reading of expository text. The Reading Teacher 39(6), 564-570.

Sample chart:

K - W - L Chart		
WHAT I ALREADY KNOW	**WHAT I WANT TO LEARN**	**WHAT I LEARNED**
Example: *Percents are used for tips.*	Example: *How do you calculate percents?*	Example: *Convert a percent into a decimal and multiply, or use a shortcut.*

COMPLETED

■ **Guided Journal Reflection and Discussion.** After significant learning in a content area, draft a few metacognitive questions and ask students to respond to them in their journals. Use the **Guided Journal Reflection and Discussion** chart, which follows, to plan this activity. After students complete their entries, facilitate a discussion of how students learned (a teacher admission can help start the discussion, if necessary). Students will likely benefit from each other's strategies and experiences.

■ **Peer Sharing/Tutoring.** After new learning, ask students to free write for a few minutes about the processes they use to complete specific tasks — such as calculating percents or writing paragraphs. Next, pair students up, and ask students within pairs to teach each other the processes they use to complete the task. If feasible — such as with percents or paragraphs — ask students to verbalize their thinking as they actually complete the task. Encourage students to ask questions of one another as they teach each other their strategies. Use the **Peer Sharing/Tutoring** chart, which follows, to plan this activity for your students. After students complete the activity, facilitate a discussion of what they learned from one another.

TOPIC/SKILL	GUIDED JOURNAL REFLECTION AND DISCUSSION
JOURNAL QUESTIONS:	Example: *What did you find most challenging about _____ (topic/skill)? How did you overcome these challenges? Where do you still need help?*
DISCUSSION QUESTIONS:	Example: *Who is willing to share what they found most challenging about _____ (topic/skill) and to tell us how they overcame the challenge?*
PLANNING NOTES:	

TOPIC	PEER SHARING/TUTORING
SKILL:	Example: *Calculating percents*
PLANNING NOTES:	
POSSIBLE DISCUSSION QUESTIONS:	Example: *Did you find that you think in similar or different ways when you calculate percents?* *How can you use what you learned from your partner when you calculate percents in the future?*

6 **Additional Activities.** Teachers and professional journals are terrific resources for learning about activities that build student comfort with questioning and encourage metacognitive reflection. They can also be good sources of ideas for ways to use student questions. Use the **Activities Suggested by Others** chart, which follows, to record these and adapt them to your needs. In the same spirit, you will likely find that the content you teach inspires you to develop original ideas that are worth sharing with others. Use the **My Ideas for Activities** chart, which also follows, to begin developing these.

Activities Suggested by Others	
SOURCE	ACTIVITY NOTES

My Ideas for Activities	
TOPIC	ACTIVITY NOTES

PART IV

PLANNING A LESSON SUPPORTED BY QUESTIONS

By now, you likely have a fuller understanding of the benefits of directing student learning using planned questions, and of the importance of teacher and student attitudes and classroom climate to successful questioning and discussion. Both teachers and students benefit from planned questioning that is targeted to specific instructional purposes. By considering in advance the learning goals you have for your students, your students' needs and interests, the wording of your questions, the cognitive processes they evoke, and the difficulty of your questions relative to your students' abilities, you increase the likelihood that your questions will engage students and achieve your intended objectives.

The questions you ask in your classroom should clearly indicate to students the thinking tasks you wish them to perform, as well as the content you wish them to use. They should be easily understood, and ought to be supported by alternative wordings and lower-level questions that lead up to them. A lack of planning can defeat your purposes. If students are unsure of what your questions ask them to do, they may not respond to them. Or, their responses may take discussion in another direction — one not intended by you — and you may miss the opportunity to engage them in your objective.

Part IV of this minicourse is designed to guide you in planning a lesson that is supported by purposeful questions. Before planning your lesson, you review the qualities of authentic questions and consider the importance of precise wording. Word banks and question stems are provided to help you reflect on word choice. Then, Related Activities take you through the steps of the lesson planning cycle.

OBJECTIVE:

- PLAN A LESSON SUPPORTED BY QUALITY QUESTIONS, TARGETED TO SPECIFIC INSTRUCTIONAL GOALS, AND DESIGNED TO ENGAGE STUDENTS IN LEARNING.

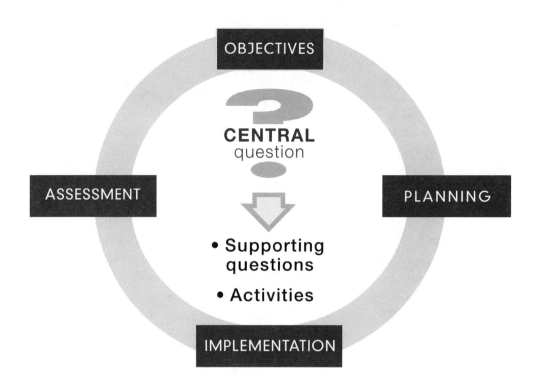

THE LESSON PLANNING AND IMPLEMENTATION CYCLE

You start by determining the topic and objectives of your lesson and drafting a **central question** that captures the main outcome you intend for this lesson. Then, as shown above, you work backward from your central question by preparing **supporting questions** and planning **activities** that will prepare your students to respond to your central question. Decide how you will assess students' responses to the central question. Finally, implement the lesson.

Related Activities in Part IV also ask you to focus on at least one aspect of the lesson that allows you to practice leading a discussion. For this purpose, you plan a central discussion question, as well as a series of probing questions to scaffold the discussion. A checklist is provided to help you review — and if needed, revise — all of your questions.

Next, you reflect on potential obstacles you identified in Part III and plan a few strategies for overcoming them. In addition, you consider students' potential responses and how you will assess their participation. Before implementing the lesson, you may also wish to review your lesson plan with other teachers to gather additional tips and advice.

At this point, you are about to begin practicing all you have learned about effective questioning and discussion, including the interpersonal skills that can help you elicit productive responses from your students. There is much for you to synthesize and apply. As you try out the techniques and strategies you have identified to advance your teaching practice, remember to use wait time to help both you and your students internalize these new processes. By moving thoughtfully, you increase the likelihood that both your students and your planned lesson will be successful.

Effective Instructional Questions

The lists that follow are intended to help you review the many qualities of effective instructional questioning and effective instructional questions before implementing a new questioning strategy with your students.

Research[15] indicates that the following questioning practices support student achievement:

■ taking time to phrase questions clearly

■ asking questions rooted in academic content

■ using appropriate wait time before asking for student responses

■ encouraging and probing student responses

■ calling on nonvolunteers as well as volunteers

■ guiding students who give incorrect responses in rethinkir

■ asking students to clarify, support, and extend their ide

■ positively reinforcing correct responses but using p
and purposefully

In addition, effective questions:

■ are interesting to students

■ are targeted to difficulty levels that are a

■ ask students to perform a variety of thinking ta

■ support student learning by scaffolding a sequentia

■ challenge students to uncover new content and mine nev

■ inspire discussion of multiple possibilities and ideas

■ respect all students' beliefs and intelligence

■ build students' awareness of their thinking and learning processes

Read 101-112
Develop or model
lesson - use it with
your students
receive feedback
via peer interaction

[15]Wilen, W., & Clegg, A. (1986). Effective questions and questioning: A research review. Theory and Research in Social Education, 14(2), 153-61.

WEAK INSTRUCTIONAL QUESTIONS

The content and phrasing of your questions determine their effectiveness in reaching specific learning objectives and motivating student thinking. Some questions that are in our adult vocabularies make poor instructional questions. They may leave students confused about what they have been asked to do and set students up for incorrect responses. Their inability to respond to these questions can leave students feeling that they have failed and can make them suspicious of further questions. Some examples of poor instructional questions are described below.

- Questions that are vague (e.g., "What do you think about _____?") leave students unsure of what they are to do and leave the accomplishment of learning goals to chance.

- Trick questions (e.g., those intended to lead students to a foregone, incorrect response) can make students feel foolish and can betray their trust.

- Questions that are too advanced or abstract for students' levels of development fail to engage students and may make them feel incapable of learning.

- Yes-and-no questions fail to challenge students; they test factual recall rather than advance student learning.

- Fill-in-the-blank questions — like yes-and-no questions — lead students in recitation and fail to engage them in thinking and learning.

WORDING OF QUESTIONS

The clearer and more precise your questioning language, the more likely it is that students will see the specific purposes of your questions.

It is important that the wording of your questions provides students with specific cues that indicate the work they are to do in response to them. If your students are to accomplish the learning goals you set for them, they must have clear signals that tell them what you intend. Your wording can provide them with these important signposts. The clearer and more precise your questioning language, the more likely it is that students will see the specific purposes of your questions.

Instructional questions are generally composed of three parts:

1. Question stems (e.g., "How can you...?" "What kind of...?") frame your questions by employing questioning words — most often, the interrogatory pronouns "who," "what," "when," "where," "why," or "how."

2. The verbs you choose — such as *compare*, *observe*, *describe*, *classify*, *distinguish*, *imagine*, and so on — indicate to students the thinking tasks they are being asked to perform.

3. Finally, the content you wish students to think about is usually presented as the subject ("How are [subject] and [subject] alike?") or object ("How would you classify [object] and [object]?") of your questions.

While it is not important that you fully understand the grammar of your questions, it is important that you attend to each of these three elements when you compose your questions. It is also important to be as specific as possible in your word choice, and to consider the vocabularies of the students who will respond to your questions, so that students can focus quickly on the task and content you intend. In addition, your questions should be worded in a way that is simple and clear — not burdened by overly complex introductions or sentence structure — so that they may be easily understood by students.

Whether you are new to instructional questioning or refining your skills, you may find the word banks presented on the pages that follow useful when composing your questions. These word banks can help you find the vocabulary you need to frame questions targeted to specific instructional purposes. They can also help you monitor the kinds of questions you ask of students — by highlighting, for example, words you use frequently and words you rarely use. They may inspire you to try new question types. As you practice and refine your questioning strategies, you will likely encounter question stems, verbs, and content phrases that are particularly effective with your students. The chart provided in Related Activities at the end of this section can help you create your own word bank.

Bloom's Taxonomy of Cognitive Skills

Bloom's taxonomy provides a tiered way of examining the variety of thinking tasks that students may be asked to perform at each level of cognitive difficulty. This word bank can be helpful when planning questions targeted at specific cognitive levels, as well as in planning a series of questions intended to lead students through multilevel thought processes — beginning, say, with recalling, then applying, and ultimately evaluating.

COGNITIVE SKILL QUESTIONS			
COGNITIVE LEVEL	**QUESTION STEM**	**THINKING TASK[16]**	**CONTENT TYPE**
LOW LEVEL:			
KNOWLEDGE	What do you…? Who do you…?	observe, recall, recognize, remember	concepts, definitions, facts, problems, processes, objects, rules, vocabulary
	How would you…? How could you…? How might you…?	arrange, chart, collect, define, describe, identify, label, list, locate, name, quote, repeat, reproduce, show, tell	
COMPREHENSION	How would you…? How could you…? How might you…?	compare, contrast, describe, demonstrate, differentiate, discuss, explain, indicate, interpret, provide examples of, predict, say in your own words, summarize, translate	concepts, definitions, facts, problems, processes, objects, rules, vocabulary
APPLICATION	How would you…? How could you…? How might you…?	alter, apply, arrange, calculate, change, choose, classify, compute, demonstrate, determine, employ, estimate, extend, figure out, illustrate, modify, predict, relate, reverse, show, solve	concepts, problems, processes, rules

[16]Several words appear in banks at more than one cognitive level, due to the many levels of complexity a single word can elicit. For example, at the application level, a student might be able to "predict" an event based on his/her concept knowledge, while predicting the results of an experiment would require analysis.

COGNITIVE LEVEL	QUESTION STEM	THINKING TASK	CONTENT TYPE
HIGH LEVEL:			
ANALYSIS	How would you...? How could you...? How might you...?	analyze, arrange, categorize, classify, compare, connect, contrast, deduce, differentiate, discriminate, dissect, distinguish, examine, explain, hypothesize, infer, investigate, predict, research, separate	concepts, events, objects, organisms, phenomena, problems, processes, rules
SYNTHESIS	How would you...? How could you...? How might you...?	build, combine, compose, conduct, connect, construct, create, develop, design, devise, draft, envision, generalize, imagine, incorporate, integrate, invent, formulate, modify, organize, plan, prepare, propose, rearrange, rewrite, set up, substitute, support, teach, test, theorize, use, write	demonstrations, ideas, experiments, evidence, models, performances, positions, products, rules, theories
	What can you...?	conclude, deduce, infer from, predict	
EVALUATION	How would you...? How could you...? How might you...?	appraise, argue for/against, assess, choose, compare, conclude, contrast, convince, decide, defend, discriminate, evaluate, explain, grade, judge, measure, rank, rate, recommend, select, score, support, test	conclusions, demonstrations, experiments, evidence, ideas, merits, performances, positions, products, theories, usefulness, value

Managing Students as They Work

The word bank that follows can help you frame the questions you use to manage independent or group work, facilitate discussion, or probe students' responses.

	MANAGEMENT QUESTIONS	
Teacher Task	**Question Stem**	**Thinking Task**
Manage, monitor	Do you...?	agree, have a plan, need help, understand the question
	Have you...?	begun to, come to an agreement on, completed, decided how you will approach, divided responsibilities, finished, taken a position
Clarify	Can you...?	define, explain, provide examples of, repeat, rephrase
Orient	What...?	does the question ask, does the task specify, are the key words
	Where can you...?	find, learn, see
	How can you... ?	determine, find out, learn, show, prove
Refocus	You said _____, but the question is _____; can you...?	rethink, reconsider, relate your ideas to, think of another way
Probe	What does...?	look like, remind you of, suggest to you
	What would...?	happen if
	How would you...?	feel if
Extend	Can you...?	predict what would happen, suggest another possibility, think of a similar situation
Narrow	Can you...?	determine what's missing, develop a rule, draw a conclusion
	What might that...?	mean, represent, suggest
Summarize	How would you...?	encapsulate, list, outline, paraphrase, say in your own words

THINKING ABOUT THINKING

This word bank can help you form questions that can help make students more aware of the ways in which they learn, reach conclusions, and evaluate content, while also considering the phases in which students arrive at metacognitive learning.

METACOGNITIVE TASK	METACOGNITIVE QUESTIONS	
	QUESTION STEM	WORD BANK
RECOGNIZE	What did you...?	do, learn, notice, think
	How did you...?	arrive at, choose, compare, connect, decide, determine, evaluate, feel, imagine, link, plan, proceed, solve
REFLECT	How did that...?	change, affect, impact, help, hurt
	What can you...?	change, do differently next time, do in addition, do instead, do to accomplish
	How can you...?	change, check, find out, help, know, learn, remind yourself, resolve, revise, solve, strengthen, support, think differently, verify
	How would you...?	explain, feel, react, teach
APPLY	What if you...?	asked a friend, asked for feedback, proceeded in steps, reminded yourself that, reversed it, slowed down, speeded up, tried again
MONITOR	What did you...?	change, do differently, learn, notice, think
	How did you...?	evaluate, feel, imagine, improve, plan, proceed

ACTIVE LISTENING QUESTION STEMS

The sentence stems that follow can help you word your active listening questions in ways that are nonthreatening to students.

Active Listening Skill	Question Stem
PARAPHRASING...	So, you're saying... is that correct? In other words... ? What I'm hearing then is... is that right? What I hear you saying... am I understanding you correctly? From what I hear you say... does that seem right to you? I'm hearing many things... do I understand your main point? As I listen to you I'm hearing... is that what you mean?
CLARIFYING[17]...	Would you tell me a little more about...? Let me see if I understand... is that correct? I'd be interested in hearing more about... It would help me understand if you'd give me an example of... So, are you saying/suggesting...? Can you tell me what you mean when you...? Can you tell me how that idea is like (different from)...? To what extent...? I'm curious to know more about... can you add to what you said? I'm intrigued by... can you tell us more? I'm interested in... how/what/why? I wonder... what do you think?
REFLECTING...	What's another way you might...? What would it look like if...? What do you think would happen if...? How was... different from (like)...? What's another way you might...? What sort of an impact do you think...? What criteria did you use to...? When have you done something like... before? What do you think...? How did you decide... (come to that conclusion)? What might happen if...?

[17]Note: Remember that asking students why they think something tends to elicit a defensive response.

ASSESSING STUDENT PARTICIPATION AND UNDERSTANDING

When planning your questions, you will also want to consider how you will judge the quality of student responses. For example, how will you know when the question has been fully addressed? What aspects of the content under discussion will you want students to minimally address before ending the discussion? What will you look for to measure student understanding? Considering these things in advance will help you weigh, support, direct, and evaluate student responses as well as compose appropriate guiding questions during discussion.

In addition to determining the qualities of *good* responses, you may also wish to anticipate ways students could *mis*understand the question or content, and how such misunderstandings could impact discussion. Before you implement your lesson, consider common misconceptions students have about the content — and possible misinterpretations of your questions — as well as how you will react to such responses.

For several reasons — such as the dynamic nature of discussion, the fact that each student may respond to or contribute a different element of the discussion, and the role that personality plays in making a contribution — discussion generally does not lend itself to formal assessment. However, discussion does provide opportunities for you to informally assess student progress and understanding and to monitor students' participation.

The information you gather during discussion can be helpful later when providing students with feedback on their efforts and when assessing students' learning and overall performance. In addition, the evidence you gather can provide important feedback for you about how well your questions are serving student learning.

The information you gather during discussion can be helpful later when providing students with feedback on their efforts and when assessing students' learning and overall performance.

Related Activities, which follow, suggest ways you can gather information about student understanding during discussion and monitor the system you use for calling on students fairly. In Part V, you will use this information to assess the progress you made in advancing your practice.

ACTIVITY NOTE

Consider your current level of proficiency with questioning and discussion before completing the activity below. Remember, your growth should be incremental. For example, if your proficiency with this skill is at the Basic level or lower (see the level-of-performance scale offered in Part I), you would be wise to use questioning to support one or two elements of a lesson. On the other hand, if you use questioning strategies at the Proficient level or above, you may be ready to build an entire lesson with questions.

Related Activities

Directions: The following activities are intended to help you plan a lesson supported by quality questions, targeted to specific instructional goals, and designed to engage students in learning. The activities should be completed sequentially and in a manner conducive to your own individual learning style.

COMPLETED

1 Think back on the professional goals you identified in the **My Goals for Questioning Skills** chart in Part I. Using **My Minicourse Journal**, which follows, use steps 1a through 1g to plan a lesson supported by questions that can help you achieve your goals.

1a. Decide a **Topic** and determine the **Objectives**[18] of the lesson you plan to teach. What is it that you would like your students to accomplish?

1b. Prepare a **Central Question** that captures the main outcome you intend. Take care to word your question clearly and to target a level of cognitive difficulty that is appropriate to your students' current stage of development.

1c. Now, think about what your students will need to learn before arriving at an answer to the question you prepared in step 1b. Starting from what they know now, prepare a series of **Supporting Questions**, the

[18]The standards your district uses for your subject and grade level can help you define your objectives.

Before writing questions, consider the thinking processes required to answer them. Remember to use verbs that identify specific thinking tasks for students. If necessary, consult the discussion of question types in Part II or the word banks in Part IV.

COMPLETED

answers to which will lead them to the intended outcome. Depending on your lesson, you may also wish to plan **Supporting Activities** (readings, projects, group activities, presentations, demonstrations, etc.) to help students answer some of these questions.

1d. Focus now on a **Discussion Question**. Prepare three versions of the question in case students do not understand it right away.

1e. Plan a few **Probing Questions** to support your **Discussion Question**.

1f. Review (and if necessary, revise) the questions you have prepared. It may be helpful to consider the following questions:

- Are your questions authentic? Interesting? Challenging?

- Have you planned a range of questions that draw on significant cognitive processes?

- Do your questions build on one another and lead to your Central Question?

- Are your question stems, verbs, and content phrases specific and clear?

- Do your questions respect students' abilities, needs, and interests?

- Do your questions pose any problems or challenges for particular students?

1g. Consider possible student responses to your questions. What information, concepts, or problems should students identify? What misconceptions and misunderstandings may they encounter? List the **Qualities of Good Responses** and the **Qualities of Misdirected Responses**.

2 Think back on the goals you identified in the **My Goals for Climate and Attitudes** chart in Part III. Now, consider the behavioral objectives you have for your students as they relate to the lesson you are planning. What behaviors will tell you that you have achieved your goals? Would you like to see increased student engagement? Longer and more thoughtful responses? Increased student comfort with sharing ideas? Greater student-to-student interaction? Using the **Behavioral Objectives** chart, which follows, list the behaviors you hope to see students exhibit during the lesson in the *Objective* column. List the strategies you will use to elicit these behaviors — such as communication skills, attitudes, and environment changes — in the *Strategies* column.

3 What role will student questions play in your lesson? Using the **Student Questions** chart, which follows, plan when you will ask students to frame questions. Consider the types of questions that you would like students to frame as well as the purpose for which you will use their questions.

COMPLETED

4 Prepare an **Informal Assessment Chart** to help you gather evidence of student learning and participation during the lesson. One way to do this is to prepare a seating chart and make multiple copies of it. Each time you facilitate a class discussion, date and label it. Alternatively, create a table that lists students' names alphabetically in rows, as shown below, so that dates of discussion can be entered as column headings; you can make multiple copies of this as well.

Sample chart:

INFORMAL ASSESSMENT CHART			
STUDENT NAME	MONTH / DAY / YEAR	MONTH / DAY / YEAR	MONTH / DAY / YEAR	MONTH / DAY / YEAR

5 Use the **Codes for Assessing Student Responses** chart, which follows, to plan how you will record the evidence of student learning and participation that you gather during the lesson. For example, you may want to use a simple system — such as check-minus, check, and check-plus — to record student participation during discussion. In addition, devise a list of abbreviations that can help you quickly and informally assess the quality of students' contributions. For instance, you could use a "U" to mean "unprepared," an "R" to indicate "took a risk," an "OT" to signify "off-topic," an "I" to note that the student's responses are improving, a "C" to record that a student is making important connections — or any other abbreviations you choose.

6 Next, consider any obstacles you identified in the **Potential Obstacles** chart in Part III and plan the steps you will take to overcome them in the **Strategies for Overcoming Obstacles** chart, which follows. You may wish to consider the following questions:

- How will you ensure that all students participate in class discussion?

- What level of listening and respect can you expect from your students?

- What can you do to slow or increase the pace of your questioning?

- What can you do to encourage students to respond more fully?

- How can you encourage students to ask and answer questions of one another?

- What can you do to prepare for a range of potential responses?

	COMPLETED
7 Discuss your lesson plan with other teachers from the same or different professional perspectives. Record their advice in the **Tips from Other Teachers** chart, which follows, and reflect on their comments before implementing the lesson.	
8 Implement your lesson. Consider videotaping the lesson to help you assess your success later on. Alternatively, you may wish to ask an experienced teacher to observe the implementation of your lesson and to provide you with feedback.	
9 Over time, collect question stems, verbs, and content words that are particularly effective with your students in the chart labeled **My Questioning Word Bank**, which follows.	

my minicourse
Journal

1a. *Topic:*

Objectives:

1.

2.

3.

1b. *Central Questions:*

1c. *Supporting Questions:*

1.

2.

3.

4.

5.

6.

1c. *Supporting Activities:*

    1.

    2.

    3.

    4.

    5.

    6.

1d. *Discussion Questions:*

    1.

    2.

    3.

1e. *Probing Questions:*

    1.

    2.

    3.

    4.

my minicourse
Journal

1f. *Review (and if necessary, revise) the questions you have prepared, considering the questions on page 113.*

1g. Qualities of Good Responses:

Qualities of Misdirected Responses:

Behavioral Objectives

Objective	Strategies
Example: *increased student engagement*	Example: *1. Plan challenging questions that are interesting to students.* *2. Allow students to prepare to respond to questions in groups or pairs.* *3. Call on nonvolunteers first and more often.* *4. Use student questions.*

Student Questions

Instructional Opportunity:	Example: *After introducing the topic.*
Type of Questions:	Example: *Any question that truly interests them.*
Purpose of Questions:	Example: *Use during discussion to increase engagement.*
Notes:	

Codes for Assessing Student Responses

THIS ABBREVIATION...	INDICATES...
Example: ✔− ✔ ✔+	Example: *a nonresponse or an inadequate response* *an adequate response* *a strong response*

Strategies for Overcoming Obstacles

OBSTACLE	STRATEGY
Example: *students coming to class unprepared*	Example: *1. Discuss situation individually with students.* *2. Consult with students' other teachers.* *2. Hold conferences with parents.* *3. Provide some start-to-finish activities in school.* *4. Place students in groups to prepare for questioning together, but make everyone responsible for contributing to discussion.*

TIPS FROM OTHER TEACHERS:

_____

_____

_____

_____

_____

_____

_____

_____

_____

_____

My Questioning Word Bank		
QUESTION STEM	VERB/TASK	CONTENT WORDS OR PHRASES

PART V

YOUR CONTINUING PROGRESS

All endings are also new beginnings. As you look back on the thoughtful steps you have just taken to engage students more fully in their learning, you also look forward to the next step you will take to improve your questioning skill. The work you have done to prepare and implement a lesson supported by questions is an important step in the advancement of your teaching practice, and it also maps the way to possible future advancements.

In Part V of this minicourse, checklists prompt you to reflect on the successes and challenges you encountered while implementing your new instructional strategies. Related Activities guide you in reflecting on what you learned from the endeavor, as well as in a constructive self-assessment of your performance. In charts that are provided, you document evidence of student learning and your own professional advancement to support your self-assessment. Finally, while the experience is fresh in your mind, you take notes that may later help you set goals for your next incremental advancement.

As noted throughout this workbook, building your capacity to question and facilitate discussion requires facility in many areas of teaching. Skilled questioning requires knowledge of different types and levels of questions; awareness of the kinds of questions you regularly ask in your classroom; understanding of students; and sensitivity to students' needs and interests. Questioning is a skill that requires a great deal of flexibility. Successful questioners use a variety of question types for varied purposes — to challenge students intellectually, gently probe their thinking, seek clarification of their responses, and encourage metacognitive reflection. Further, proficient questioning involves *planning* of questions and activities intended to lead students toward important understandings, as well as spontaneous but careful *responsiveness* to students to help

> Successful questioners use a variety of question types for varied purposes — to challenge students intellectually, gently probe their thinking, seek clarification of their responses, and encourage metacognitive reflection.

OBJECTIVES:

- **REFLECT ON AND SELF-ASSESS IMPLEMENTATION OF LESSON SUPPORTED BY QUESTIONS.**

- **CELEBRATE SUCCESSES!**

- **PLAN NEXT STEP FOR GROWTH IN USING QUESTIONING.**

them arrive at these understandings on their own. For this reason, questioning also depends on facility with numerous communication and interpersonal skills. Successful questioners strive to create a positive and supportive classroom climate, use wait time judiciously, encourage multiple perspectives and participation of all students, and positively reinforce student responses.

Due to the wide-ranging proficiency on which questioning skill depends, it is important to remember that developing skill in this area takes time. This minicourse encourages you to work toward increased proficiency a step at a time and to allow yourself ample practice with the dynamic processes described. The first steps you take toward increasing your proficiency in this area will likely highlight the complexity of the questioning process. This learning is critical to your advancement, so be sure to recognize it as a success. Before undertaking your next planned advancement, remember to celebrate any progress you have made. Your appreciation of the complex task before you, your willingness to proceed a step at a time, and your recognition of your incremental advancements will refresh and recharge you for your next journey through the learning cycle.

REFLECTING ON THE IMPLEMENTATION OF YOUR PLANNED LESSON

Part I of this minicourse introduced the level-of-performance scale associated with the use of questioning and discussion techniques in *Enhancing Professional Practice: A Framework for Teaching*. As you know, self-assessment is useful before you undertake new learning as well as after, so that you can measure growth attributable to your new learning. While it is not critical that you use this level-of-performance scale to assess your progress in implementing new questioning strategies, it is important that you identify the progress you have made and that you look to students for evidence of your increased proficiency. The scale is provided again on the next page for your convenience.

As noted earlier, there are many skills you can consider in preparation for self-assessing your increased proficiency with instructional questioning strategies. The level-of-performance scale provided here divides these questioning and discussion skills into three elements:

- **quality of questions**

- **discussion techniques**

- **student participation**

	LEVEL OF PERFORMANCE			
ELEMENT	UNSATISFACTORY	BASIC	PROFICIENT	DISTINGUISHED
QUALITY OF QUESTIONS	Teacher's questions are virtually all of poor quality.	Teacher's questions are a combination of low and high quality. Only some invite a response.	Most of teacher's questions are of high quality. Adequate time is available for students to respond.	Teacher's questions are of uniformly high quality, with adequate time for students to respond. Students formulate many questions.
DISCUSSION TECHNIQUES	Interaction between teacher and students is predominantly recitation style, with teacher mediating all questions and answers.	Teacher makes some attempt to engage students in a true discussion, with uneven results.	Classroom interaction represents true discussion, with teacher stepping, when appropriate, to the side.	Students assume considerable responsibility for the success of the discussion, initiating topics and making unsolicited contributions.
STUDENT PARTICIPATION	Only a few students participate in the discussion.	Teacher attempts to engage all students in the discussion, but with only limited success.	Teacher successfully engages all students in the discussion.	Students themselves ensure that all students participate in the discussion.

Figure 5.1. A Level-of-Performance Scale for Questioning and Discussion Skills

The checklists on the following pages provide questions that are intended to help you reflect on the elements that influence proficiency in questioning and discussion. Depending on your level of proficiency prior to planning your lesson — and thus, the extent to which your planned lesson was supported by questions — some questions may not apply to you yet. As you consider each checkpoint, try to recall specific evidence of student success (such as student behaviors you observed, work samples, specific student responses, and so forth) to help you weigh your own success with each element.

QUALITY OF QUESTIONS

☐ *Were my questions appropriate to students' present abilities?*

☐ *Did my questions adequately reflect my objectives?*

☐ *Did I plan an adequate range of question types to accomplish my objectives?*

☐ *Did my questions adequately challenge students?*

☐ *Did my questions adequately interest and engage students?*

☐ *Was the series of questions I planned adequate to lead students from their present understanding toward my objectives?*

☐ *Did I plan adequate supporting questions to lead students toward my objectives?*

☐ *Were my questions clear and understandable to students?*

☐ *Did students' responses indicate that they understood what they were being asked to do?*

☐ *Were my questions respectful of and sensitive to individual students' personal circumstances and abilities?*

☐ *Did I compose effective follow-up questions based on students' responses?*

☐ *Did I use questions to effectively probe, clarify, and extend students' responses?*

☐ *Did I use questions to check students' understanding?*

☐ *Did my questions encourage metacognitive reflection?*

☐ *Did my questions help students achieve the outcome I intended?*

DISCUSSION TECHNIQUES

☐ *Did adjustments I made to my physical classroom environment facilitate class discussion?*

☐ *Were ground rules effective in promoting listening and respect among students?*

☐ *Were the strategies I used to call on students successful? (Did I wait to call on students until after I framed my questions? Did I call on nonvolunteers as well as volunteers?)*

☐ *Did I use student names fluently to moderate discussion?*

☐ *Did I use adequate wait time before asking for student responses?*

☐ *Did I use adequate wait time after students responded?*

☐ *Did I address students in a polite and friendly manner?*

☐ *Did I use active listening skills — such as mirroring, paraphrasing, clarifying, and reflecting — to encourage student responses?*

☐ *Did I use nonverbal cues — such as eye contact, body language, and facial expressions — to encourage student responses?*

☐ *Did I positively reinforce student responses?*

☐ *Did I use my listening skills to compose appropriate next questions or to direct follow-up activities?*

☐ Was discussion satisfying and complete?

☐ Was I receptive to all points of view?

☐ Did I encourage multiple points of view?

☐ Did I ever take sides? Impose my opinion? Provide an answer that may not be true? Express frustration?

☐ Did I respond to surprising responses in an appropriate manner?

☐ Did I encourage students to respond to one another while I remained in the background?

☐ Did I encourage students to ask as well as answer questions?

☐ Did the discussion lead students to the objective I planned?

STUDENT PARTICIPATION

☐ Were students ready for the level of questioning I introduced? (Or could students have benefited from additional practice opportunities?)

☐ Did students have adequate time and content preparation to respond to my questions?

☐ Did I plan adequate activities to support my questions and lead students to the learning outcome I identified?

☐ Did most students participate in discussion?

☐ Were student responses generally on task?

☐ Did students respond positively to my active listening and probing by elaborating their responses?

☐ Was any student embarrassed as a result of responding, or being unable to respond, to a question?

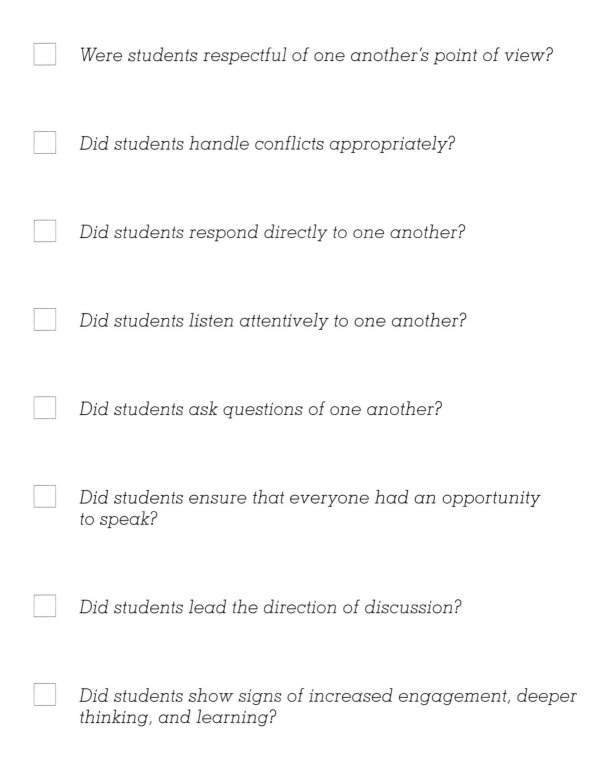

☐ Were students respectful of one another's point of view?

☐ Did students handle conflicts appropriately?

☐ Did students respond directly to one another?

☐ Did students listen attentively to one another?

☐ Did students ask questions of one another?

☐ Did students ensure that everyone had an opportunity to speak?

☐ Did students lead the direction of discussion?

☐ Did students show signs of increased engagement, deeper thinking, and learning?

SELF-ASSESSING YOUR CURRENT PROFICIENCY

After reflecting on the elements that influence proficiency in each area, you may wish to organize your reflection by considering the elements in a given area in sum. After weighing the elements in one area together, you may wish to apply the level-of-performance scale provided earlier to evaluate your current proficiency as follows:

1 — unsatisfactory

2 — basic

3 — proficient

4 — distinguished

As noted in Part I, the "unsatisfactory" level is used to describe a performance that demonstrates little or no understanding of how questioning skill can be used to advance student learning. The "basic" performance level indicates an understanding of the ways questioning can be used in the service of student learning, but an inconsistent level of success in implementing questioning strategies. The "proficient" level represents solid, consistent use of questioning to advance student learning. And the "distinguished" level describes success in the formation of a true community of learners between the teacher and students — one in which all students are engaged with the teacher's provocative questions and in which students ask and answer questions of each other in a respectful and purposeful manner.

... teachers who achieve a proficient level of skill in any given domain understand that, during daily practice, all components are interdependent and interwoven.

It bears repeating that level-of-performance scales momentarily isolate an aspect of teaching practice in order to reflect upon it and assess your strengths, as well as areas for advancement. However, teachers who achieve a proficient level of skill in any given domain understand that, during daily practice, all components are interdependent and interwoven.

PLANNING FUTURE ADVANCEMENT

The final step before repeating the learning cycle outlined in this minicourse is using your self-assessment to begin planning the next steps of your professional development. As you review the checklists of skills and behaviors that contribute to successful instructional questioning, you will likely feel satisfied with some areas of your practice and find that there are others you wish to improve. By taking notes and outlining plans now, you can begin sketching a map to guide your future professional growth.

> By taking notes and outlining plans now, you can begin sketching a map to guide your future professional growth.

For instance, as you scan the checklists provided in Part V, you may find that there is something you would do differently the next time you implement a lesson supported by questions. Or, there may be another strategy you would like to explore more fully or deeply. Perhaps you already know what content you wish to explore the next time you plan a lesson supported by questions and can note questions, ideas, and approaches that are already forming in your thoughts.

Jot down any and all aspects of your practice that you wish to refine — whether you will attend to these in your next learning cycle or later. Take some time to sort your long-term professional goals from your next steps. Also, consider the scope of your plans and how you can achieve them incrementally.

Later, when you repeat the learning cycle, you can review your notes before setting a new goal for your professional advancement. When that time arrives, you may follow your map exactly, or you may journey in an unanticipated direction. It matters not. Whether you see the path before you or behind you, the process of continually reflecting on and assessing your progress will pave your way to enhanced professional practice and improved student learning.

The PATHWISE Minicourse Learning Cycle

STAGE I
Gather and reflect on new information; begin to self-assess your practice.

STAGE II
Consider the skill more deeply; reflect on your current teaching practice; set an incremental learning goal.

STAGE III
Examine related issues that support the skill; prepare students for the new approach you will use with them.

STAGE IV
Create and implement a lesson plan in which you rehearse the skill at a new level.

STAGE V
Reflect on your new learning; take notes that form the basis of your next incremental advancement.

Directions: The following activities are intended to help you self-assess the implementation of your planned lesson and your current proficiency with questioning and discussion, as well as to help you plan your next step for growth in this area. The activities should be completed sequentially and in a manner conducive to your own individual learning style.

		COMPLETED
1	Using **My Minicourse Journal**, which follows, record and elaborate on your self-assessment of your current proficiency with questioning and discussion, which you completed earlier in Part V. Questions are provided to guide your reflection.	
2	Think back on the goals you identified in the **My Goals for Questioning Skills** chart in Part I. Did you achieve your goals? Using the **Analysis of My Goals for Questioning Skills** chart, which follows, note the progress you have made in each area, as well as the evidence that supports your conclusion.	
3	Think back on the instructional objectives you listed in **My Minicourse Journal** in Part IV. Did you achieve your instructional objectives for this lesson? Using the **Instructional Analysis** chart, which follows, note the evidence of student learning you observed for each objective.	

4 Think back on the goals you identified in the **My Goals for Climate and Attitudes** chart in Part III. Did you achieve your goals? Using the **Analysis of My Goals for Climate and Attitudes** chart, which follows, note progress you have made in each area, as well as the evidence that supports your conclusion.

5 Think back on the behavioral objectives you listed in the **Behavioral Objectives** chart in Part IV. Did you achieve your behavioral objectives for this lesson? Using the **Behavioral Analysis** chart, which follows, note the evidence of student behavior you observed for each objective.

6 Think back on the questions you asked during your lesson and consider students' responses. What do the responses tell you about students' thinking and learning? Using the **Analysis of Student Learning** chart, which follows, reflect on this question.

7 Think back on the potential obstacles you identified in the **Potential Obstacles** chart in Part III. Did you make progress against the obstacles you anticipated? Using the **Analysis of Potential Obstacles** chart, which follows, note the progress you have made against each obstacle, as well as the evidence that supports your conclusion.

8   Use the **Question Analysis** chart, which follows, to analyze any questions you planned that elicited unintended responses or no response from students. Write the question in the column labeled *Original Question*. Then, in the *Question Type/Purpose* column, describe the question in any way that seems useful (for example, note Open or Closed, describe the level of student thinking it required, or note your purpose for asking it). Under *Student Response*, paraphrase or describe students' reactions to the question. Finally, under *Revised Question*, write a new version of the question to try next time.

9   You may find it useful to discuss the implementation of your lesson with other teachers. If you videotaped your lesson, consider showing it to a more experienced teacher and asking for his/her feedback. If you are a member of a study group, consider sharing this experience with questioning and discussion and asking others to share their experiences. If your lesson was observed by another teacher, reflect on his/her feedback. Record what you learned in the **What I Learned From Other Teachers** chart, which follows.

	COMPLETED
10 In the space entitled **My Next Steps**, which follows, reflect on questioning and discussion skills you wish to advance when you repeat this minicourse. These notes may be useful to you later when you begin planning your next inquiry-based lesson plan. Questions are provided to guide your reflection.	
11 When you are ready to plan your next lesson, repeat the Related Activities provided throughout this minicourse. Remember to consider the notes you drafted in **My Next Steps**, above. Review earlier sections of the minicourse as you reflect on any challenges you face. *Congratulations on your achievements!*	

my minicourse
Journal

Date: _____   Current Level of Proficiency: _____

What are your questioning strengths?

Which questioning skills do you need to develop further?

How have you enhanced your proficiency in using questioning as an instructional strategy?

What changes do you see in your students as a result of your enhanced proficiency?

What did you learn from attempting these new strategies?

Analysis of My Goals for Questioning Skills

GOAL	PROGRESS	SUPPORTING EVIDENCE
Example: *I would like to be able to develop questions that really make my students think.*	Example: *Students were initially unwilling to question the book's apparent reverence for Native American culture and values. But the questions I asked about the text and characters led students to notice gaps between what was said and how characters behaved, then to work to understand the gaps.*	Example: *Students said Cooper appreciated Native American culture and values. When asked to provide evidence of this, however, they most often pointed to Hawk-Eye, who is not a Native American. They concluded that while Cooper shows appreciation for Native American values, he and/or his audience may not have been able to embrace the idea of a main character who was a Native American.*
1.		
2.		

GOAL	PROGRESS	SUPPORTING EVIDENCE
3.		
4.		
5.		

INSTRUCTIONAL OBJECTIVE	EVIDENCE THAT OBJECTIVE WAS ACHIEVED
Example: *Students will better understand the nineteenth-century view of Native American culture and values expressed by Cooper in The Last of the Mohicans.*	Example: *1. Students' own questions helped unearth "gaps" in the book's perspective (e.g., "Why do Chingachgook and Uncas rarely speak?" "Where does Hawk-Eye get his name?")* *2. Once students were willing to see beyond the reverential attitudes on the surface, they had some amazing revelations ("It's as if Hawk-Eye is Native American, when he is not.").* *3. Through discussion, students determined that, while the book reveres Native American values, Native American characters are not well developed and do not have central roles.*
1.	
2.	
3.	

GOAL	PROGRESS	SUPPORTING EVIDENCE
Example: *I would like to increase the number of students who contribute to class discussions.*	Example: *By changing my approach to calling on students, more students participated; by using probing strategies, I was able to help them articulate their ideas. Greater input from students made the discussion much spicier and helped students achieve the objective for the lesson.*	Example: *1. Called on many students who do not normally volunteer; they responded!* *2. Called on nonvolunteers first, which produced a greater variety of ideas.* *3. Noticed students who do not normally speak up raising their hands and called on them.*
1.		
2.		

GOAL	PROGRESS	SUPPORTING EVIDENCE
3.		
4.		
5.		

Behavioral Objective	Evidence That Objective Was Achieved
Example: *enhance student engagement*	Example: 1. *Started discussion using student-generated questions written at the beginning of the lesson.* 2. *Strategies for calling on students increased number of responses.* 3. *Questions helped students unearth a mystery and begin asking their own questions.* 4. *Questions on the table really provoked students and most of the class worked together to answer them.*
1.	
2.	
3.	
4.	

QUESTION	STUDENT RESPONSE	WHAT THE RESPONSE SAYS ABOUT STUDENT THINKING/LEARNING
Example: *How would you describe the view of Native Americans Cooper expresses in* The Last of the Mohicans?	Example: *Students were unanimous that the book supports Native American culture and values. When I asked for evidence, they protested, "Why? It's so apparent!"*	Example: *Students tend to want to believe in the good around them, which made it hard for them, at first, to approach this novel with skepticism. Like adults, students need to explore "the facts" more closely before they can see "shades of gray" in meaning — in this case, early nineteenth-century obstacles to writing about Native American culture.*

Analysis of Potential Obstacles

Obstacle	Progress	Supporting Evidence
Example: *Several of my students continually come to class unprepared. How can I motivate them to take an interest in learning and contribute to class discussion?*	Example: *1. Consulted with students' parents, informed them of the problem, and enlisted their support.* *2. Consulted with students' other teachers; one recommended assigning activities to the student that do not depend on preparation but begin to get the student involved.* *3. Noticed that the overall level of student engagement with questions made these students more attentive in class.*	Example: *1. _____ has been more attentive since my conference with his parents.* *2. Used a question drafted by _____; her level of attention increased during discussion of her question and she made some tentative contributions during group work.*
1.		
2.		

OBSTACLE	PROGRESS	SUPPORTING EVIDENCE
3.		
4.		
5.		

Question Analysis			
ORIGINAL QUESTION	**QUESTION TYPE/PURPOSE**	**STUDENT RESPONSE**	**REVISED QUESTION**
Example: *What do you think about Hawk-Eye?*	Example: *Type: Open-ended, analysis* *Purpose: Trying to get students to recognize that Native American values are expressed through a non-Native American character.*	Example: *Students responded by telling me how they felt about Hawk-Eye. Question needs to be more specific.*	Example: *How do Hawk-Eye's skills compare to those ascribed to Native Americans during this time period?*

What I Learned From Other Teachers	
TEACHER	INPUT

MY NEXT STEPS

Which questioning skills would you like to focus on the next time you use this minicourse?

_____

_____

_____

_____

_____

_____

Which lesson would you select when you repeat the minicourse?

_____

_____

_____

_____

_____

_____

_____

Planning notes:

_____

_____

_____

_____

_____

_____

_____

Appendix A:
A Framework for Teaching

Domain 1
PLANNING AND PREPARATION

1a: Demonstrating Knowledge of Content and Pedagogy

Knowledge of content
Knowledge of prerequisite relationships
Knowledge of content-related pedagogy

1b: Demonstrating Knowledge of Students

Knowledge of characteristics of age group
Knowledge of students' varied approaches
    to learning
Knowledge of students' skills and knowledge
Knowledge of students' interests and
    cultural heritage

1c: Selecting Instructional Goals

Value
Clarity
Suitability for diverse students
Balance

1d: Demonstrating Knowledge of Resources

Resources for teaching
Resources for students

1e: Designing Coherent Instruction

Learning activities
Instructional materials and resources
Instructional groups
Lesson and unit structure

1f: Assessing Student Learning

Congruence with instructional goals
Criteria and standards
Use for planning

Domain 2
THE CLASSROOM ENVIRONMENT

2a: Creating an Environment of Respect and Rapport

Teacher interaction with students
Student interaction

2b: Establishing a Culture for Learning

Importance of content
Student pride in work
Expectations for learning and achievement

2c: Managing Classroom Procedures

Management of instructional groups
Management of transitions
Management of materials and supplies
Performance of noninstructional duties
Supervision of volunteers and paraprofessionals

2d: Managing Student Behavior

Expectations
Monitoring of student behavior
Response to student misbehavior

2e: Organizing Physical Space

Safety and arrangement of furniture
Accessibility to learning and use of
    physical resources

Figure A1. Components of Professional Practice

Domain 3	Domain 4
INSTRUCTION	**PROFESSIONAL RESPONSIBILITIES**

Domain 3

INSTRUCTION

3a: Communicating Clearly and Accurately

   Directions and procedures
   Oral and written language

3b) Using Questioning and Discussion Techniques

   Quality of questions
   Discussion techniques
   Student participation

3c: Engaging Students in Learning

   Representation of content
   Activities and assignments
   Grouping of students
   Instructional materials and resources
   Structure and pacing

3d: Providing Feedback to Students

   Quality: accurate, substantive, constructive,
      and specific
   Timeliness

3e: Demonstrating Flexibility and Responsivenes

   Lesson adjustment
   Response to students
   Persistence

Domain 4

PROFESSIONAL RESPONSIBILITIES

4a: Reflecting on Teaching

   Accuracy
   Use in future teaching

4b: Maintaining Accurate Records

   Student completion of assignments
   Student progress in learning
   Noninstructional records

4c: Communicating with Families

   Information about the instructional program
   Information about individual students
   Engagement of families in the instructional program

4d: Contributing to the School and District

   Relationships with colleagues
   Service to the school
   Participation in school and district projects

4e: Growing and Developing Professionally

   Enhancement of content knowledge and
      pedagogical skill
   Service to the profession

4f: Showing Professionalism

   Service to students
   Advocacy
   Decision making

Figure A1. Components of Professional Practice

Appendix B: Resources[19]

General

Appalachia Regional Educational Laboratory. *How better questioning leads to improved learning.* Available: http://www.ael.org/rel/quilt/questng.htm

Bloom, B., Englehart, M., Furst, E., & Krathwohl, D. (Eds.). (1956). *Taxonomy of educational objectives. Handbook 1: Cognitive domain.* New York: David McKay.

Chuska, K. (1995). *Improving classroom questions: A teacher's guide to increasing student motivation, participation, and higher-level thinking.* Bloomington, IN: Phi Beta Kappa Educational Foundation.

Costa, A. (1984). Mediating the metacognitive. *Educational Leadership, 42*(3), 57-62.

Gall, M. (1970). The use of questions in teaching. *Review of Educational Research, 40*, 707-721.

Gall, M. (1984). Synthesis of research on teachers' questioning. *Educational Leadership, 42*, 40-47.

Honea, J., & Mark, J. (1982). Wait-time as an instructional variable: An influence on teacher and student. *Clearing House, 56*(4), 167-70.

Larson, B. E., (1997, March). *Teachers' conceptions of discussion as method and outcome.* Paper presented at the annual meeting of the American Educational Research Association, Chicago, IL. (ERIC Document Reproduction Service No. ED 407 692)

Morgan, N., & Saxton, J. (1991). *Teaching, questioning, and learning.* New York: Routledge.

Rosenshine, B., Meister, C., & Chapman, S. (1996). Teaching students to generate questioning skills for teachers: A review of intervention studies. *Review of Educational Research, 66*(2), 181-121.

Wilen, W. (1991). Questioning skills for teachers: *What research says to the teacher (3rd ed.).* Washington, DC: National Education Association. (ERIC Document Reproduction Service No. ED 332 983)

Wilen, W., & Clegg, A. (1986). Effective questions and questioning: A research review. *Theory and Research in Social Education, 14*(2), 153-61.

---

[19]This resource list is intended as a starting place for teachers' efforts to locate articles on questioning that are appropriate to their individual practices. However, educators using the minicourse are responsible for previewing and selecting materials that best meet the needs of their schools and communities. Presentation of these resources does not represent endorsement by Educational Testing Service of the points of view represented in the articles.

ELEMENTARY SCHOOL

LANGUAGE ARTS

Harvey, S. (1998). *Nonfiction matters: Reading, writing, and research in grades 3-8* [see Part 1]. Portland, ME: Stenhouse.

National Education Association. *Reading matters: Question-answer relationships* [grades 3-8]. Available: http://www.nea.org/readingmatters/class/question.html

Raphael, T. (1982, November). Question-answering strategies for children. *The Reading Teacher, 36*(2), 186-190.

Raphael T. (1986, February). Teaching question-answer relationships, revisited. *The Reading Teacher, 39*(6), 516-522.

SOCIAL STUDIES

Short, K. G., Schroeder, J., Laird, J., Kauffman, G., Ferguson, M. J., & Crawford, K. M. (1996). *Learning together through inquiry: From Columbus to integrated curriculum.* Portland, ME: Stenhouse.

Sunal, C. S., & Haas, M. E. (2002). *Social studies for the elementary and middle grades: A constructivist approach* [see chapters 3 & 5]. Boston, MA: Allyn & Bacon.

Zarrillo , J. J. (2000). Inquiry: Challenging students with discovery learning and problem solving. In *Teaching elementary social studies: Principles and applications.* Upper Saddle River, NJ: Prentice Hall.

MATHEMATICS

Hoyles, C. (1985). What is the point of group discussion in mathematics? *Educational Studies in Mathematics, 16*, 205-14.

Garlikov, R. (n.d.). *The Socratic method: Teaching by asking instead of telling* [third grade]. Available: http://www.garlikov.com/Soc_Meth.html

SCIENCE

Lewis, M. L. (1993). *State of the art: Transforming ideas for teaching and learning science: A guide for elementary science education.* Washington, DC: U.S. Dept. of Education, Office of Educational Research and Improvement, Office of Research. Available: http://www.ed.gov/pubs/StateArt/Science/

Synergy Learning International (Pub.). (2000, March/April). Connect: Inquiry learning [Special issue]. Connect Magazine, 13(4). Available: http://www.exploratorium.edu/ifi/ resources/classroom/connect/

Elstgeest, J. (1985). The right question at the right time. In W. Harlen (Ed.), *Primary Science: Taking the plunge: How to teach primary science more effectively* (pp. 36-46). Portsmouth, NH: Heinemann.

MIDDLE SCHOOL

LANGUAGE ARTS

Moeller, M. V., & Moeller, V. J. (2000). *The middle school English teacher's guide to active learning.* Larchmont, NY: Eye on Education. Available (for purchase): http://www.eyeoneducation.com

SOCIAL STUDIES

Sunal, C. S., & Haas, M. E. (2002). *Social studies for the elementary and middle grades: A constructivist approach* [see chapters 3 & 5]. Boston, MA: Allyn & Bacon.

MATHEMATICS

Hoyles, C. (1985). What is the point of group discussion in mathematics? *Educational Studies in Mathematics, 16*, 205-14.

Driscoll, M. (1999). *Fostering algebraic thinking: A guide for teachers grades 6-10* [ISBN: 0-325-00154-5]. Portsmouth, NH: Heinemann.

Reinhart, S. (2000, April). Never say anything a kid can say. *Mathematics Teaching in the Middle School, 5*(8), 478-483.

Boyle, R. A., & Skopp, L. (1998). Teachers as inquirers: Constructing a model of best practice. (ERIC Document Reproduction Service No. ED 417 981) Available: http://www.educ.sfu.ca/narstsite/conference/98papers.htm [scroll to bottom of page]

Swift, N., & Gooding, C. (1983). Interaction of wait time feedback and questioning instruction on middle school science teaching. *Journal of Research in Science Teaching, 20*, 721-30.

Yei, C-J., Wang, K-H., & Huang, S-C. (1998, April). A comparative study on the use of questioning strategies between beginning teacher and experienced teacher [biology]. Paper presented at the annual meeting of the National Association for Research in Science Teaching, San Diego, CA.

Synergy Learning International (Pub.). (2000, March/April). Connect: Inquiry learning [Special issue]. Connect Magazine, 13(4). Available: http://www.exploratorium.edu/ifi/ resources/classroom/connect/

Taines, C., Schneider, R., & Blumenfeld, P. C. (2000, April). Observations of urban middle school students engaged in technology-supported inquiry. Paper presented at the annual meeting of the American Educational Research Association, New Orleans, LA. Available: http://www-personal.umich.edu/~krajcik/taines.pap.pdf

HIGH SCHOOL

ART

College Entrance Examination Board. (1985). *Academic preparation in the Arts: Teaching for transition from high school to college.* New York: Author.

Getzels, J., & Csikszentmihalyi, M. (1976). *The creative vision: A longitudinal study of problem finding in art.* New York: Wiley.

LANGUAGE ARTS

College Entrance Examination Board. (1985). *Academic preparation in English: Teaching for transition from high school to college.* New York: Author.

Conner, A., & Chalmers-Neubauer, I. (1989). Mrs. Schuster adopts discussion: A four-week experiment in an English classroom. *English Education, 21*, 30-38.

Haroutunian-Gordon, S. (1991). *Turning the soul: Teaching through conversation in the high school.* Chicago: University of Chicago Press.

Moeller, V. J., & Moeller, M. V. (2000). *The high school English teacher's guide to active learning.* Larchmont, NY: Eye on Education. Available (for purchase): http://www.eyeoneducation.com

Schaeffer, J. (Winter 1987). When students come to ask questions. *Academic Connections,* 8-11.

Wolf, D. P. (Winter, 1987). The art of questioning. *Academic Connections,* 1-7. Available: http://www.exploratorium.edu/IFI/resources/workshops/artofquestioning.html

SOCIAL STUDIES

Atwood, V. A., and Wilen, W. W. (1991).Wait time and effective social studies instruction: What can research in science education tell us?" *Social Education, 55,* 179-81. (ERIC Document Reproduction Service No. EJ 430 537)

Dillon, J. T. (1981). Discussion characteristics in a sample of religion and social studies classes. *Character Potential: A Record of Research, 9,* 203-205.

Hess, D. (2001). *Teaching students to discuss controversial public issues.* Available: http://www.indiana.edu/~ssdc/cpidig.htm

Kelly, T. (1989). Leading class discussions of controversial issues. *Social Education, 53,* 368-370.

MATHEMATICS

Hoyles, C. (1985). What is the point of group discussion in mathematics? *Educational Studies in Mathematics, 16,* 205-14.

Driscoll, M. (1999). *Fostering algebraic thinking: A guide for teachers grades 6-10* [ISBN: 0-325-00154-5]. Portsmouth, NH: Heinemann.

Silver, E. A., Kilpatrick, J., & Schlesinger, B. (1990). *Thinking through mathematics: Fostering inquiry and communication in mathematics classrooms.* Educational Equity Project.

Chang, K. E., Lin, P. C., & Sung, Y. T. (2000). Socratic-dialectic learning system of recursion programming. *Journal of Educational Computing Research, 23*(2), 133-50.

College Entrance Examination Board. (1990). *Academic preparation in science: Teaching for transition from high school to college.* New York: Author.

Fasching, J., & Erickson, B. (1985). Group discussions in the chemistry classroom and the problem-solving skills of students. *Journal of Chemical Education, 62*, 842-846.

Hake, R. R. (1992). Socratic pedagogy in the introductory physics lab. *The Physics Teacher, 30*, 546-552.

SPECIAL NEEDS

Campbell, D. (1986). Developing mathematical literacy in a bilingual classroom. In J. Cook-Gumperz (Ed.), *The social construction of literacy.* New York: Cambridge University Press.

Evans, M., & Bienert, H. (1992). Control and paradox in teacher conversations with shy children. *Canadian Journal of Behavioral Science, 24*, 502-16.

Paris, S. G. (1990, Nov./Dec.). Promoting metacognition and motivation of exceptional children. *Remedial and Special Education*, 7-15.

Rich, R. Z., & Blake, S. (1995). Collaborative questioning: Fostering the self-regulated learner. *LD Forum, 20*(2), 38-40.

Wood, H., & Wood, D. (1984). An experimental evaluation of the effects of five styles of teacher conversation on the language of hearing-impaired children. *Journal of Child Psychology and Psychiatry, 25*, 45-62.